The Call to Follow Jesus

Studies in the Gospel of Mark

From the Series *Kingdom Living in a Twisted World*

Kim Laliberte

WestBow
PRESS
A DIVISION OF THOMAS NELSON

WestBow Press books may be ordered through booksellers or by contacting:

WestBow Press
A Division of Thomas Nelson
1663 Liberty Drive
Bloomington, IN 47403
www.westbowpress.com
1-(866) 928-1240

Because of the dynamic nature of the Internet, any web addresses or links contained in this book may have changed since publication and may no longer be valid. The views expressed in this work are solely those of the author and do not necessarily reflect the views of the publisher, and the publisher hereby disclaims any responsibility for them.

Any people depicted in stock imagery provided by Thinkstock are models, and such images are being used for illustrative purposes only.

Certain stock imagery © Thinkstock.

Scripture quotations taken from the New American Standard Bible®, Copyright © 1960, 1962, 1963, 1968, 1971, 1972, 1973, 1975, 1977, 1995 by The Lockman Foundation. Used by permission." (www.Lockman.org)

ISBN: 978-1-4497-9592-4 (sc)
ISBN: 978-1-4497-9591-7 (e)

Library of Congress Control Number: 2013909249

Printed in the United States of America.

WestBow Press rev. date: 6/21/2013

DEDICATION

No one writes a book in a vacuum. Everyone we meet and interact with becomes part of our story. For those of us who love to communicate by the written word, the people who touch us or teach us become part of the warp and woof of our writing. Hundreds of people have touched my life and encouraged me to write – too many to recount. I trust you know who you are. For years I chose not to believe you until, by the sheer number of people and the gentle Voice always speaking, I finally understood that God was calling me to this task.

I want to thank my pastor of 24 years, Mark Hopper for asking me to help him prepare sermon study notes on his preaching of the gospel of Mark and for believing so much in the intelligence and creativity of his staff that he encouraged every one of us to write for publication.

This book is dedicated to:

- My church family and the women and leadership teams of the Diamond Bar Evangelical Free Church for their prayers, encouragement, loving nudges and sometimes outright nagging to, "get writing!" Thank you!
- To my son Jonathan, who is in his own right an excellent communicator and solid man of God.
- To my husband John, the most amazing man of my acquaintance. A man of many talents, he is also my editor, encourager, comforter, best friend and focuser -- the one who kept pulling me back from all my other projects and interests to, "Get the book written first!" Thank you, beloved.
- To my precious Lord and Savior, Jesus Christ, the Name that is above all names. It is about Him I must write. To Him be the Glory!

Kim Laliberte,

August, 2012

TABLE OF CONTENTS

INTRODUCTION

I'm thrilled you have chosen to pick up this book on the gospel of Mark and trust you will not be disappointed as you go through the chapters and learn how twelve men went from being followers of Christ, to disciples, to world changers.

Exposure to Jesus Christ will change our lives. Everywhere we turn in the gospels when people encounter Christ, lives are changed. Disciples are grounded in their faith, sick are healed, the multitudes are amazed, demons are cast out, and men and women are challenged to seek first the kingdom of God. As we launch into this incredible journey of the life and land of Jesus be prepared to be transformed.

This may be the first time you have read and interacted with a book like this. I intend to go straight through the gospel of Mark in a verse by verse method. Scholars call it the *expository method*. I am no scholar but my years of studying Scripture in many different ways has convinced me that this is the best way to learn what God is saying. You might find this method a bit stretching but stay with it.

You will begin to learn for yourself how and why the Scriptures are grouped the way they are. As you see Jesus and His disciples in the context of the culture and the time in which they lived, you will be able to connect your own experiences to what Jesus said and did. Before you begin, please consider the following suggestions as you engage in this study:

Note to EBook Readers

You won't have a paper workbook in front of you, but that should not be a problem. Those who have tested the study in an e-format have suggested a number of ways to study the material:

1) Answer the questions in your head and jot down notes to remember in a note-taking app or in the appropriate place in your e-Bible.

2) If you are paper person, write down answers or thoughts to remember in a notebook or journal.

3) Hand-write thoughts to remember directly in your Bible.

4) I would love to hear from you on ways you develop to study the material. Contact me at my website, www.kimlaliberteministries.com, with your ideas and suggestions.

The Sections of each Chapter (for all readers):

1) Be sure to read the *Background Information*. Jesus lived in a different day, time, and culture than ours. Reviewing the background information will help you understand those differences. I have done some of the work for you by digging out facts about the time and the location. And you may even get a hint or two on some of the answers to the questions!

2) Pay particular attention to *The Disciples Perspective*. This section provides clues to being a disciple of Christ by summarizing what the disciples saw, heard, thought and did. It can also help you think through your own journey as His disciple.

3) Don't pass on the *Historical Quotes*. History is, after all, His Story and throughout history, as my pastor Mark Hopper has said, "God uses people to bring people to Christ." Quotes by those who have made it through have encouraged and strengthened me in my entire walk with Christ. Every morning I read with a pencil in my hand hoping to find something from the past or from others further along than I that will encourage me and others in the now.

4) Optionally read the *Parallel Passages* in Matthew, Luke and John to gain further depth and insight into Mark's account. In some places I recommend that you read a parallel passage when it clarifies what Mark is saying.

5) The sections entitled *Getting to the Heart of the Matter* are an important part of the book. The descriptions and questions listed there will help you interact with the Scripture itself and learn principles to apply to everyday living. These questions are designed to challenge people at all stages of their faith-walk. Some questions may seem either too easy or too difficult to answer. Please don't be intimidated or put off by this if you find some questions too hard. Just try your best or skip questions you can't answer. We are all at different stages of following Him and I encourage you to not give up. Whenever your life intersects with the Word of God and you are open to what He has for you in it, you will learn something. Answer the questions you feel able to answer and feel free to "pass" on questions you are uncomfortable with – or, if you're up for a challenge, give them a try. Don't stress over getting the "right" answer. Saturating yourself in the Scripture is what is important.

On the other hand, if you find a question that is too easy, go for it – pick up your ipad™, ipod™, pc, mac™ or just a good old fashioned Bible study help book and get to work. You will be amazed at what God reveals as you search out hidden treasures and nuggets of truth. Whether you share them in a group is not as important as what He is giving you. He never wastes anything. If you are faithful, He will take what you've learned and allow you to bless someone someday in some way. And it may be just the thing you need to hear at this particular time in your own life.

On occasion you will be asked to look up verses in different parts of the Bible, though they relate closely to Mark's gospel. Studying these verses will help you understand the context of the book, sheds light on what Mark is saying in his gospel, and helps illuminate important, practical matters that can directly impact your walk.

6) At the end of each chapter's study is a short section called *Family Matters*. Films and movies are large communication tools in today's culture and they speak to our culture in ways no other medium can. I choose to recommend things from this medium and others such as a song that has touched our family in some way through the years. We have found in raising our son movies can be good teachers when seen and discussed together. Of course, you are the arbiter of what is appropriate for your own family. I encourage you to check things out before blindly following my recommendation. And, by the way, you should make this a habit of your life in other areas as well. God's Word is the only completely trustworthy message. All of the rest of us preachers, teachers, authors, movies makers, song-writers, artists and others are just, as I learned a long time ago, "one beggar sharing bread with another." His Word alone is true Truth!

Finally, let me encourage you as you follow along through the chapters, to continually consider these three questions and make them a part of your study routine:

1) **What do you *observe* about Jesus' interaction with others?**

2) **What principles can you *absorb* from studying this section?**

3) **What does Jesus do that you can *imitate* in your life today?**

How to Use This Book

Each chapter is divided into five sections or *days*. If this is to be used with a women's study where the group and the women leaders are comfortable with the "five day week study" format, by all means use it in this way. However, if it is to be used in a small group, Life Group or Adult Bible Fellowship format where the group may not have as much time available to do all the sections in a week, feel free to divide the study into smaller parts.

You can choose either a section or two a week or a study pace that will best suit the needs of the group. Because it is a verse by verse study, no formula needs to be followed. That being said, it is best to have a plan to begin and end the study. If this is an individual or group study, determine how long you will take to go through this gospel study and stick to that schedule.

If your group chooses not to do homework due to busy schedules or for whatever reason, I suggest that a group leader go over the questions before the meeting and become at least familiar with them. The verses can be looked up and questions answered when the group meets.

My prayer for you as I write this today is that you will be changed and transformed more into His likeness because you have said *yes* to this study. He knows who you are and He is already working in you to prepare you! Welcome to kingdom living!

Kim Laliberte
San Diego, CA
December, 2012

Chapter 1
The Call of the Voice of Authority (Mark 1)

Day 1
Defining the Call (Mark 1:1–8)

As you read the paragraphs below that contain a brief historical reference point during which the gospel of Mark was written, think about parallels comparing today with the situation in Mark's day.

Background Information

At about the time the gospel of Mark was written (approximately AD 50–80, with most scholars favoring AD 65–70), Emperor Nero was on the throne of Rome (AD 54–68). The gospel is believed to have been written primarily to Roman Christians during these times when Rome was in chaos.

After five years of responsible ruling, Nero went mad and was out of control. He placed heavy taxes on the estates of citizens who were childless. He made false accusations as a basis for confiscating entire fortunes of many citizens. He "invited" people to commit suicide at public banquets, took over the Roman Senate, and made slaves of the senators.

Early in his reign, Christians were left alone to worship in their own way, just as other religious groups in the city were free to worship in their way. However, in AD 64, a fierce fire swept through the city and raged for over a week, destroying much of the city. Many believed Nero had the fire started. (You may have heard the phrase, "Nero fiddled while Rome burned.") Needing a scapegoat, Nero turned on the Christians, having them arrested and tortured. Dressed in animal skins, Christians were torn to pieces by wild dogs, used as torches at Nero's garden parties, or thrown to wild beasts in the arena.

Peter was also writing his letters (1-2 Peter) at this time to infuse courage into the suffering church. Mark, who was connected to Peter as either a disciple or his interpreter, followed, writing an account depicting Jesus' life as a servant-king who came to earth, suffered, died, and rose victorious, giving hope to the young church. The gospel of Mark spoke to the suffering believers in Rome. They were reduced to a catacomb existence, fleeing the city, or facing martyrdom. An account of Jesus' life who, "came to do the will of Him Who sent Me," (John 6:38) was a strong encouragement to the beleaguered saints.

Finally, Mark kept Jesus' mission to usher in the kingdom of heaven (kingdom of God) (Mark 1:14–15) in the forefront of his readers' thinking.

It took years of my own Christian experience to understand what the kingdom of heaven was really about. I was already living it out in my walk but didn't understand the basics of kingdom living:

- A kingdom must have a ruler (God).

- His will is the rule of the kingdom.

It's that simple. Either He is in charge as He lives out His rule in me, or I am in charge and set up my own kingdom in opposition to His. When Jesus directs us to pray, "Thy Kingdom come," (Matt. 6:10) He doesn't mean we pray it into existence. Instead, "We pray for it to take over at all points in the personal, social, political order where it is now excluded."[1] In other words, the kingdom of heaven is now present as we act upon the power of God within us to bring healing to our world in all areas.

Disciples' Perspective
A deeper study of the gospel of Mark can help us re-orient our lives to bring the gospel (or message) of our lives into alignment with Christ's life. Mark learned what Christ could do for a person who trusted Him completely and unswervingly. Really knowing Christ gives meaning and purpose to difficulties and failures. As we seek to make the gospel our own, everything that happens—every experience we have that illuminates our inadequacy and God's sufficiency—is part of forming the gospel in us.

Historical Quote
"I have a great need for Christ. I have a great Christ for my needs" (Count Nicholas von Zinzendorf, c. 1768).

Getting to the Heart of the Matter
Today's Reading: Mark 1:1–8
Parallel passages: Matt. 3:1–12, Luke 3:1–20, John 1:19–28

The author of Mark is actually unknown, though it is generally accepted that John Mark (*John* being his Hebrew name and *Mark* being his Roman surname) is the author. His commonly used name was Mark, which may indicate that his main

---

[1] Dallas Willard, *The Divine Conspiracy* (San Francisco: HarperCollins, 1998)

The Call to Follow Jesus

sphere of influence was in the Gentile world. We first meet him in Acts 12:12 in connection with a prayer meeting at his mother's house.

He was probably born while Jesus was still alive and may have been a teenager when Christ was crucified.[2] Some scholars believe he may also have been present in the garden of Gethsemane when Jesus was arrested.

1. **Let's identify who is in Mark's world. Review the following passages and record what you learn about Mark. Identify every person who knows him, and write down what is said about him:**

   (a) Acts 15:37–39

   (b) 1 Peter 5:13

   (c) 2 Timothy 4:10–11

   (d) Colossians 4:10

2. **In your own words, define a disciple. You may need to look up the word in a dictionary or Bible dictionary.**

3. **Write down your thoughts on the differences between a mentor and a model.**

> **The Greeks were swayed by argument, reason, and intellectual thinking, but the Roman mind was focused on swift action and power, oppressing and conquering other people. According to Irving Jensen, "Mark shows incessant confrontation of Jesus with the religious leaders and the multitudes. The leaders always opposed Jesus ..."**

There are four different gospels written to four different groups. Matthew was written to the Jews and other religious people and presented Jesus' life from the point of view of the coming Messiah and King. Mark was written to the Romans and presented Jesus as the Servant coming to do His Father's will. Luke presented Jesus as the Perfect Man (100 percent man) and was written primarily to Gentiles. John was written to the entire world and presented Jesus as God (100 percent God) having come in the flesh.

4. **The word *gospel* has both Jewish and Roman roots and means "good news." In Rome, the word was often used to announce events about the emperor's life. In this context, what does Mark's use of the word in Mark 1:1 mean?**

---

[2] Irving Jensen, *Jensen's Survey of the New Testament*, (Chicago: Moody Press, 1981), 134

5. **When a dignitary was coming to a certain region, a messenger went ahead to prepare the way. Read Malachi 3:1 and Isaiah 40:3–5. What does each passage say about God's messenger?**

6. **What characteristics do you observe from Mark 1:1–8 about John the Baptist as a person?**

7. **Write down what you observe about John's ministry from reading Mark 1:1–8.**

When I started law school, even though I had some familiarity with terminology from my days as a paralegal, it was like being thrown into a foreign country without a guidebook. I had to learn a whole new language known primarily in the legal world and completely foreign to the general masses. To some people uninitiated in Christianity, words that are basically understood by most believers may exclude Christ-seekers (unbelievers) as much as legal terms exclude non-lawyers. When you speak to Christ-seekers about your relationship with Christ, it is easy to slip into "Christian-ese," thus excluding or putting off the person you are speaking with.

8. **Rewrite the following words in terms a Christ-seeker can understand. (You may need to look this up in a Bible dictionary to familiarize yourself with the term, or just try to define the word from the context of the verses surrounding the text.)**

    (a) Repentance (1:4)

    (b) Forgiveness (1:4)

    (c) Confessing sin (1:5)

    (d) Baptism (1:5)

9. **Mark 1:5 explores the lengths to which people went to meet Jesus. The people wanted something more than rules and religion. People still want more today. They want relationship, not religion. Blaise Pascal is generally believed to have said that there is a "God-shaped vacuum in the heart of every man that only He can fill."[3] How can we become a**

---

[3] This phrase has been alternatively attributed to Augustine.

people or a church that helps people find relationship with Christ, thus filling the vacuum, rather than just religion?

10. **Jerusalem is about twenty miles from the Jordan River and approximately four thousand feet above it. The people in Jesus' time walked a long way out and a long way up to get to Jesus. How far and how long are you willing to search to find deeper relationship with Him?**

As you move through this study, watch for and record clues to developing a deeper walk with Jesus. Observe the slow but dogged progress of the disciples as they tried to follow Jesus who promised to make them "become fishers of men." (Mark 1:17)

Day 2
Baptism and Temptation (Mark 1:9-13)

I read recently about a traveler who was hunting in South America. While walking through the forest, he was drawn to the sound of agitated birds. He approached the sound and watched, fascinated, as a pair of birds were anxiously fluttering over a nest of eggs. The traveler then saw the problem: a highly poisonous snake was slithering up the tree toward the nest.

Suddenly, the male bird flew away and was observed flapping around a nearby bush as though anxiously looking for something. The man watched as the bird returned to the nest and laid a small, leafy twig over the nest. The two birds then flew to a higher branch to watch as the snake slithered inevitably forward. Just as the snake prepared to strike, it suddenly threw back its head, recoiled, and writhed away down the tree. The pair of birds burst into rapturous song.

The traveler, intrigued, climbed the tree and removed the twig. When he later asked the natives about it, he was told that it was from a bush that was deadly to the snake; the very sight and odor would cause any snake to flee. The helpless bird knew the bush and in an hour of danger used the bush to protect the nest.[4] In today's lesson, Jesus models how He protects Himself from temptation of the enemy by knowing the Word of God and wrapping it around Himself.

---

[4] J. Sidlow Baxter, *Awake, My Heart.* (London/Edinburgh: Marshall, Morgan & Scott, LTD., 1959), 36

Background Information

Part of Jesus' ministry was to break Satan's control over humanity. (Isa. 61:1-4) His call to be baptized signified a beginning, an awakening of Messiah to His role and His ministry of reconciliation. (1 Cor. 12:13)

The gospel of John excludes information about Jesus' baptism and temptation probably because John's gospel portrays Jesus as God. Likewise, Mark gives only a few verses on Jesus' temptation while other gospels give the topic much more attention.

After being baptized, Jesus was immediately driven by the Spirit into the desert. There He was tempted by Satan. It was in the midst of these trials that Jesus had to make choices between God's best and the world's best. Everything He went through was an example to help us live out our own struggles as people of His kingdom.

Disciples' Perspective

It was not until after Jesus' baptism and testing in the desert that He called His first disciples. It is safe to assume that some of those who would be future disciples might have been present at Jesus' bapstim. It was not until after Jesus' baptism and testing in the desert that He called His first disciples. Scripture records that many followers of John left him to follow Jesus and in the next section we will learn that some of Jesus' future disciples were already acquainted with Him when they received the call.

Historical Quote

I never saw a moor,
I never saw the sea,
Yet I know how the heather looks,
And what a wave must be.
I never spoke with God,
Nor visited in heaven,
Yet certain am I of the spot
As if the chart were given.
                -Emily Dickinson

> The Greek word for *immediately* is *enthus.* It means, "Straightaway, without hesitation or lingering." Some scholars surmise that Mark's use of the word *immediately* is a way of communicating to believers the immediacy of God's power in response to the needs of humanity. It is mentioned forty-one times in the book of Mark.

Getting to the Heart of the Matter

Today's Reading Mark 1:9-13
Parallel Passages: Matt. 3:13-17, Luke 3:21-22, John 1:29-34; Matt. 4:1-11, Luke 4:1-13

1. **Review Mark 1 and underline the following words (and their derivatives or words having the same meaning):**

(a) Amazing

(b) Authority

(c) Immediately

(d) Wilderness

2. **What do each of these words tell you about: (a) Jesus' ministry? (b) The act of becoming a disciple?**

3. **Read Mark 1:9-11. Why do you think the author only gives three verses to this important moment in Jesus' public ministry? (Hint: Think about what you have learned in this study so far.)**

4. **Read the parallel passages (Matt. 4:1-11, Luke 4:1-13). What details can you add to Mark's narrative from reading the above passages?**

5. **The entire Godhead (Father, Son, Holy Spirit) are involved in Jesus' mission to save the lost. How do you see the Godhead at work in Mark 1:9-11? Describe anything you see from the passage about their individual roles in Jesus' earthly mission.**

6. **List all who were present at Jesus' baptism.**

7. **Why do you think Jesus was baptized?**

The wilderness is thought by some scholars to stretch between Jerusalem and the Dead Sea and was commonly known as "the devastation" or "the rolling bad lands." Measuring 35 by 15 miles, the place was made of limestone and large jagged rocks. It was a barren, chalky soil covered with tiny pebbles. Under the Middle Eastern sun it was like a furnace.

Perhaps because of the persecution Roman Christians were experiencing during the time Mark was writing, he mentions wilderness or wild beasts more than once in Mark 1:1-13. This is one theme of Mark. Many citizens were forced to flee their homes either out of the city altogether or into the catacombs. Mark pictures Jesus' temptation in the desert as overcoming the wilderness.

8. **Read Mark 1:12-13. Think about your own life today. What is your wilderness like? What temptations are you and/or your family facing? How does knowing that Jesus overcame the loneliness, horror and danger of the wilderness help you today?**

9. Scripture reveals that Jesus was tempted 'in all ways as we are' (Heb. 4:15). From your review of the parallel passages to Jesus' temptation, how was He tempted in the following areas?

   (a) The Flesh
   (b) Pride
   (c) Power
   (d) Greed

10. In Mark 1:12 Jesus was impelled by the Spirit into the wilderness immediately after His baptism. Notice the contrast between where His temptation took place (the desert) and where Adam's temptation took place (the garden). Do you think this is significant? Why or why not? Write your observations.

11. List one or two temptations you are currently facing. How have your prior trials prepared you for this season of life? Being able to identify these areas is a key to a growing faith.

12. Review Isa. 61:1-4 and the parallel passage of Luke 4:14-21. If part of Jesus' ministry was to break Satan's control over humanity, how does Jesus' temptation in the desert begin to do this? Go through each verse in Isa. 61:1-4 and write down everything Jesus came to do.[5]

You have probably heard it said "You may be the only Bible someone may ever read." Jesus certainly portrayed this in His own life on earth. To me it is a frightening statement. But in a sense, maybe it is true. Each of us who carry the risen Christ in our hearts is living the gospel out through our choices, actions and words. It is seen in our attitudes, values, actions and relationships. The people around us are reading our gospel every day.

What happened to Jesus in this short treatise is what happens to us – and because it happened to Him we can take great comfort in knowing we are not alone in our temptations. He is always with us. As we grow, He will continually teach us how to protect the nest!

---

[5] We will be referring to the Isaiah 61:1-4 passage many times throughout this study. I think it is a key passage to the whole of our journey as disciples.

The Call to Follow Jesus

Day 3
Responding to the Call (Mark 1:14-20)

Background Information

The call of Simon, Andrew, and James and John the sons of Zebedee in today's reading was not their first encounter with Jesus. Mark omitted Jesus' year of early Judean ministry (John 1:15-4:42). According to John's gospel, some time earlier Andrew and an unnamed disciple (probably John) were invited to "come and see" where Jesus lived. (John 1:39). John's gospel also records that other disciples likewise knew Him before being actually called by Him as apostles. Some scholars believe that they and the others actually first became Christ-followers before being called by Christ as disciples.

According to *Training of the Twelve* [6] A.B. Bruce said, "The twelve arrived at their final intimate relation to Jesus only by degrees, three stages in the history of their fellowship with Him as the Christ…" The first four chapters of John tell how they first became *acquainted* with Him and began to accompany Him on occasion, first at a wedding in Cana (John 2:1) and at a Passover in Jerusalem (John 2:13,17,22).

In the second stage, *fellowship* with Christ, the various disciples began to spend more and more time with Jesus traveling with Him, some leaving their careers to follow Him. The third and final phase of *discipleship* began when they were chosen by Christ from the mass of His followers to be trained for the great work of apostleship. This has relevance for us today as not everyone comes to Christ in the same way. For some it is instantly on hearing, for others it may involve a journey of discovery.

Disciple's Perspective

Each of us is an indispensable link in God's continuing creation. We were born to know Him and become reproducers of our faith. Reaching one person at a time as He did and as He taught His disciples is the best way to reach the world. There can be no effectiveness in our life and ministry until we hear and respond to God's call upon us. Paul Tournier says that our task as laymen is to live our personal commitment with Christ with such intensity as to make it contagious. Are you living a contagious life?

---

[6] A.B. Bruce, *The Training of the Twelve* (Grand Rapids, Mich: Kregel Publications, 1971)

Historical Quote

"He comes to us as One unknown, without a name, as of old by the lakeside; He came to those men who knew Him not. He speaks to us the same words: 'Follow thou Me!' and sets us to the tasks which He has to fulfill for our time. He commands. And to those who obey Him, whether they be wise or simple, He will reveal Himself in the toils, the conflicts, the sufferings which they shall pass through in His fellowship, and, as an ineffable mystery, they shall learn in their own experience Who He is."

- Albert Schweitzer

Getting to the Heart of the Matter

Today's Reading: Mark 1:14-20
Parallel Passages: Matt. 4:18-22, Luke 5:1-11

Mark 1:14-15 summarizes Jesus' whole ministry in Galilee. From what you explore in today's reading, you will define the context of when His ministry began, where it happened, and the essence of what Jesus said was the basis of His ministry.

Jesus proclaims the kingdom to summon people. He stands as God's final word of address to man in man's last hour. Either man submits to the summons or he chooses the world and its riches along with the consequences of his choice. It is an either/or event. Dallas Willard in *Revolution of Character* says "…the ruined soul is not a person who has missed a few theological points and may flunk a theological exam at the end of life. Hell is not an oops or a slip. One does not miss heaven by a hair, but by constant effort to avoid and escape God."[7] How do the above comments change the way we should look at evangelism?

In Mark 1:16-17 Jesus calls to Simon, Andrew, James and John and tells them to "Follow Me." Those words invite relationship. The disciples are invited to walk the same road Jesus walked.

1. **What does Jesus' comment, "follow Me" mean to you as a modern day disciple?**

2. **What do you think it means in Mark 1:17 when Jesus says, "Follow Me and I will make you *become* fishers of men?" (italics mine).**

3. **The term "fishers of men" in Mark 1:17 in Greek literally means to "take fish alive; to catch them in such a way that they are still alive when brought to the shore." In this context, what do you think it means to "take men alive"?**

---

[7] Dallas Willard and Donald Simpson, *Revolution of Character*, (Col Springs: NavPress, 2005)

4. **Do you think some evangelistic methods today can turn people off/kill their interest? Give an example.**

5. **What can happen when new believers are immediately met with rules and regulations to keep versus the power of Christianity to change and transform?**

6. **What suggestions do you have to change the method of evangelism without changing the message?**

7. **Do you think it is realistic to tell us in our hectic lives that we should become fishers of men when we all have so many struggles, problems, time constraints and other things demanding our attention? Why or why not?**

As disciples, we are the link between God and men. When we *pray* for someone, we invite God to call them, meet them and be in their midst in whatever they are going through at that moment. When we *help* someone, we invite God to touch them through our hands, voice, and feet. When we *invite* someone, we ask them to enter into God's vicinity and be changed by Him.

8. **Why are so many people in the church today content to let the professionals do all the evangelizing? What holds people back from reproducing their faith in others?**

John the Baptist was called by God for his task. The disciples were called by Jesus to follow Him and learn how to change the world. Saul of Tarsus on the other hand was driven. He was driven to seek out and kill Christians – that is until he met Jesus and received his Call on the road to Damascus (Acts 9).

9. **Write down the difference between being called and being driven. Which word better describes your life right now?**

10. **Do you think being called means giving up your career to go somewhere or do something you have no interest in going or doing?**

11. **List some other Biblical characters who were initially driven.**

12. **God uses ordinary people to bring about His purposes. Look up Ex. 3:7-10. How does God rescue His people? What principle can you draw from this passage about life as a disciple today?**

13. **In *The Lord of the Rings*, in order to help him stay the course of his mission, Lady Galadriel tells Frodo: "This task was appointed to *you* and if you do not find a way, no one will." Is there some task that God has given to you alone that you have been putting off? Is there something you need to do that may be from the Lord? Write it here.**

One of the ways Jesus taught was by example. In a crowd, He was always thinking, watching, praying. He was alert to how God wanted to use Him in the moment and was amenable to interruptions in His daily plans. Think about how we respond to interruptions today. How would our lives change if we could develop the same attitude He did as we go about our daily business at work, the children's sporting events, helping at school or interacting with people on the street, in the church, the neighborhood or in our family?

Day 4
Who is your Authority? (Mark 1:21-39)

One Fourth of July we were with a group of friends and our thirteen year old son was enjoying swimming in the pool with his friends. Determining it was time to leave, I hollered over my shoulder "Jonathan, it's time to go." Without hesitation he instantly obeyed. "Okay, mom." And *that very second* he climbed out of the pool! There was a silence around the table as 10 pairs of eyes turned astonished looks on us. "He's getting out – just like that?" questioned one parent while others maintained an awed silence. Trying to hide my own shock, with total poise I said, "Oh, yes," as though it was a totally expected, everyday result. My husband burst out laughing and I sheepishly replied, "Actually, this is the first time it has ever happened."

When I read today's section of Scripture and see the amazement and astonishment of the people when the voice of Authority speaks I am reminded of this rather humorous story. I recall the extreme shock and amazement on the faces of our friends as the voice of authority, in this one instance, elicited instant obedience from our son.

One of the keys to how Jesus ministered is the authority He exhibited in various situations. Everyone is under some kind of authority. Even Jesus came to, "…do the will of Him who sent Me." (John 4:34)

Background Information

This section explores a very busy time in Jesus' ministry. It probably represents one day (or if using the Jewish calendar which begins at sunset, two days). Here we see Jesus busy about the Father's business which is the business of restoring men to wholeness, primarily spiritual, but occasionally physical.

Josephus describes Galilee as a land of great villages: "The cities lie very thick and the very many villages that are here are everywhere so full of people, because of the richness of their soil, that the very least of them contained more than 15,000 inhabitants." Reports about Jesus' authoritative word immediately went forth into the region. As William Lane said, "The disturbance of men by God has begun."[8]

Disciples' Perspective

All week we have been looking at the disciples' call: believe, commit, and be changed. Not much is said about the disciples in this passage but they were clearly present (Mark 1:21). They were nevertheless learning through observing Jesus as He taught with authority, touched people's lives with His healing power and showed His dependency on the Father through His times of prayer.

Part of our task as disciples is to learn from Jesus' life and follow Him. By studying the book of Mark we come up close and personal to learn how to do life as He did it. Through this study we are learning to consider how Jesus observed and looked to His Father for the next step. Today as you read, continue to observe how Jesus lived and what the disciples might be picking up by being in His presence.

Historical Quote

"I long to accomplish a great and noble task, but it is my chief duty to accomplish small tasks as if they were great and noble."
-Helen Keller

Getting to the Heart of the Matter

Today's Reading: Mark 1:21-39
Parallel passages: Luke 4:31-44; Matt. 8:14-17

Lloyd Ogilvie in *Life Without Limits*[9] says of Jesus, "He was a Messiah with a mission. He was the Master on the move. The Divine Son was about His Father's business." Review Isa. 61:1-4 and Luke 4:14-21 from Day 2. Observe how Jesus is fulfilling Isaiah 61 in today's reading.

---

[8] William Lane, *The New International Commentary on the New Testament, Gospel of Mark*, F.F. Bruce, Ed. (Grand Rapids: William. B. Eerdmans 1974, 1979)
[9] Lloyd Ogilvie, *Life Without Limits*, (Waco: Word, Inc. 1975)

The first miracle mentioned by Mark here is in the spiritual realm (the casting out of the demon from the man in the synagogue). Some scholars were of the opinion that there is evidence that demonism was rampant in the Roman Empire. Any student of world history is familiar with the multiplicity of gods worshiped in Rome in the first century. Where idols are worshiped, demons are present; thus for Mark to choose to start his gospel with this miracle is quite astute. The unspoken message of Mark's gospel is that if Jesus exercised power over the spirit realm, He had power over any realm. Secondly, it was an early indication of Jesus' Divinity. Only God has this kind of power.

Jesus' Authority Heals

1. **Read Mark 1:21-45. Consider yourself as a new disciple present with Jesus here. Write down your observations about what is happening in the following situations: (Look for: who was present; what were their responses to what *they* experienced; how did Jesus approach, respond or handle the situation; what practical lessons can you learn from each scenario?)**

   (a) **Jesus casting out a demon (:23-28)**

   (b) **Jesus healing Simon's mother-in-law (:29-34)**

   (c) **Jesus rising early in the morning to pray while it is still dark (:35-39)**

   (d) **Jesus cleansing a leper (:40-45)**

2. **Read Mark 1:21-27 and James 2:19. Look at the words used by the demons Jesus was casting out. What do you think it means when they said they knew who He was or that they believed in Him? Based on these passages would you say that believing in Jesus is enough to live a Godly life? Is it enough to get to heaven?**

3. **Compare this section with Josh. 2:8-14 (pay particular attention to 2:11). "We have heard…" may imply that not only Rahab but the whole town believed in the Lord's power. What distinguished Rahab from the rest of the town of Jericho? What does the Joshua passage say about belief?**

> Jesus used no spells or incantations to cause the demon to leave. Instead, the demon was felled with a word – the Word. The people were familiar with the incantations, but were astonished when Jesus spoke a word and was instantly obeyed.

4. In Mark 1:23-27 look at who Jesus was speaking to. What does the spirit call Jesus?

5. What happened,

    (a) to the man?

    (b) to the demon?

    (c) to the people when Jesus spoke?

6. What do you see of Jesus' credentials in the passage? Do you think it was the exorcism of the demon or the Person of Jesus that attracted the people? What does this say about how people are attracted to Christ today?

> When we work, we work. When we pray, God works.

7. What words are used to describe Jesus in Mark 1:21-27 and who uses the words?

8. What is the difference between Jesus' teaching and that of the Scribes and Pharisees in Mark 1:21-27?

> The response of the disciples shows that they too had a long way to go in their journey with Jesus. There is hope for you and me! Don't lose heart. Stand firm.

Do you know this hymn?

> "And though this world with devils filled,
> should threaten to undo us,
> We will not fear,
> for God hath willed His truth to triumph through us.
> The Prince of Darkness Grim,
> we tremble not for him;
> His rage we can endure,
> for lo, his doom is sure.
> One little word shall fell him."

This is a stanza from Martin Luther's, *A Mighty Fortress is our God*. While there is much to love and learn from contemporary music today, learning the words to the great hymns of the faith can also be a great comfort in times of trial and stress. Familiarizing yourself with music from the history of our faith can only broaden your perspective and strengthen your faith.

Jesus' Authority Restores

In *90 Minutes in Heaven*[10] Don Piper chronicles his journey from a horrific accident that left him severely disabled, his 90 minutes spent in heaven and his journey back to God after rehabilitation. In it he talks about 'the new normal' and that his life could never go back to the way it was before the accident. Over the years, so many people have been helped by the phrase 'the new normal'. In one sense, Peter's mother-in-law experienced a new normal when she was healed from a devastating fever. What areas of change that you perceive as either positive or negative in your life do you have to consider as possibly a new normal? (It may be job loss, illness, empty nests, full nests, aging parents or so many other things)

9. **Read Mark 1:29-31. What happened to Simon's mother-in-law? What was restored to her? What did she do as a result?**

10. **How did He do it? Read Mark 1:35. Look at each word/phrase in the verse. What do you learn about Jesus' method of praying? What principles can you take from this verse to help you cope with all of the things you deal with on a daily basis?**

Bill Hybels in *Too Busy Not to Pray*[11] puts it this way: "The heart and soul of the Christian life is learning to hear God's voice and developing the courage to do what He tells us to do."

11. **Read Mark 1:35-39. When the disciples found Jesus praying what was their response?**

12. **What did Jesus know and model that the disciples needed to cultivate in their own lives?**

13. **How did Jesus handle the drive to be busy?**

14. *Read Mark 1:39-45.* **In this passage we see a man in the synagogue who has been left untouched by the truth. When Jesus entered, everything changed. The man's life changed with a word and the people's lives were changed by their astonishment at a new and different way of teaching. Everywhere around us are people who need to be touched by the truth and the transforming power of Jesus to change them (and us).**

---

[10] Don Piper with Cecil Murphey, *90 Minutes in Heaven,*(Grand Rapids: Revell 2004)
[11] Bill Hybels, *Too Busy Not to Pray,*(Downers Grove: InterVarsity Press (1998), 99

Sometimes the church and believers do not "astonish and amaze" people in the same way Jesus did. Why do you think people aren't touched and healed by the Truth as the demon-possessed man was?

15. **Read 1 Cor. 12:12. The church is all about *people*. It is not a *building;* it is a body. If together we are called to gather, serve, pray and encourage, rather than criticize the church for doing a poor job, how can we be part of building a church that is astonished and amazed, filled with power to change lives?**

A recent poll asked Americans about busyness in their lives. The majority, 59 percent said, "I wish I could slow down. I wish I could cope better." Not only have I lived this scenario as a busy lawyer, wife, mother and one who ministers to women and adults, I see it every day in the strained eyes of the women I serve. As they try to juggle all the balls, meet every deadline, cook every meal, follow through on every detail, they fight discouragement. I see it when I teach adults, and men, sometimes in total frustration state, 'I can't do one more thing!'

I've seen the bewildered looks on peoples' faces when a pastor encourages them to spend time every day with Jesus. They look at him like he has two heads. And sometimes, I'm there too! Yet, truly, it is the only way. The Christian life is not about adding more things to an already impossibly busy life or doing more. It is about seeking God and hearing from Him about what are the BEST things, not just the good things.

The enemy will always try to pile on events or activities in your life to keep you from what you are called to do. But there is always time to do God's will. If you are indeed too busy, perhaps you need to examine what is on your plate. Jesus' life is a living, active model of this principle and as His disciples we must see what He saw, hear what He heard, and do what He did. And since He spent time trying to hear the voice of His Father, you and I should do no less.

Digging Deeper

If you want to understand more, I encourage you to do a word study in the Scripture on the word, *authority*. Go online or look in a Bible Concordance the word you want to study. Jot down and look at each verse that mentions the word. Determine from the verse and verses around it (context) what it can teach you. Record your findings and write down what you learn for your own life.

We must learn with the disciples that we have the same authority Jesus did since the power of His Spirit dwells within us. As you continue in this study, keep this concept in mind.

Day 5
Getting in Touch With the Gift of Pain (Mark 1:40-45)

Background Information

If you had to choose a disease would you choose one that had no pain associated with it? Many people think that would be a good choice but anyone who is familiar with Hansen's disease would never choose this option. Leprosy (also called Hansen's Disease) is a contagious disease of no pain. It begins as a small, almost un-noticeable sore which increases in size until it eats away the extremities one by one and then spreads to the brain and spinal cord. It is a terrible disease – one that is still prevalent in some parts of the world today.

Lepers have a defective pain notification system in their body. The disease acts as an anesthetic, numbing the pain cells of the hand, feet, nose, ears and eyes. Thus, the patient feels no pain but also feels no pleasure. Never to feel a friend's hug or a spouse's kiss would be a dismal life indeed.

Destruction occurs because the warning signs of pain are gone. Thus you could touch a hot stove, grab a rusting nail or walk on glass without feeling pain. Imagine what such a life would be like. Shoes wouldn't pinch; you wouldn't feel calluses as they turned into infections. Tissue would wear away exposing bone until finally the bone is worn down leaving stubs where toes once were.

Because leprosy is contagious, everything the leper touches is considered unclean (Lev. 13-14). This disease separated families because people with the disease were often considered dead to their families[12]. Some Biblical scholars have even likened the disease of leprosy to sin.

Disciples Perspective

Don't you wish you knew what the disciples were thinking as Jesus waded in to the political, social and physical world of leprosy? They were all Jews and knew the rules about staying as far away from lepers as possible. Can't you just hear Peter's private thoughts: "I hope He doesn't expect *me* to get in the midst of these kinds of situations!" Or Thomas, "Is He crazy? Maybe his family was right." Or Levi, "I didn't think I was signing on for this!" We're all there.

Sometimes God asks the impossible, the improbable or the unpopular. In our own strength? No way! But as we go deeper into kingdom living, He makes the way. He will not call you where He cannot keep you as the disciples were learning.

---

[12] Philip Yancey, *Where is God When it Hurts?* (Grand Rapids: Zondervan, 1970).

Historical Quote

"God whispers to us in our pleasures, speaks to us in our conscience, but shouts in our pains: It is His megaphone to rouse a deaf world"

-C.S. Lewis, *The Problem of Pain.*

As a young believer I often had trouble really understanding God's love for me. I never doubted that He could do something but I often doubted that He would do something for me. On the one hand, it's a cry of faith. On the other, it is a cry of one who perceives himself or herself as undeserving or unworthy. My misconception about God's intimate love and compassion for my brokenness is not unlike the scenario in today's study with the man's comment, "If you are willing…" Where are you in this discussion?

Getting to the Heart of the Matter

Today's Reading: Mark 1:40-45
Parallel passages: Matt. 8:1-4; Luke 5:12-16

1. **Read the passage and the parallel passages in Matt. 8:1-4 and Luke 5:12-14. Review the above comments in the Background Information and write down parallels of the disease of leprosy with the disease of sin. For example, Warren Wiersbe in his commentary on Leviticus 13-14[13] says that, "…like leprosy, sin is deeper than the skin; it spreads; it defiles; it isolates and is fit only for the fire."**

2. **Pick out other parallels. Use these verses to help you: Heb. 3:12-13, 1 Tim. 4:2, Rom. 6:23.**

3. **Scripture records in Mark 1:40-42 that the man was cleansed of the leprosy but doesn't mention healing. Is there is a difference? Compare this with sin. Are we ever healed from sin or are we cleansed from it?**

4. **A willingness to accept something uncomfortable can come in various disguises or misconceptions such as fatalism, fatigue, lack of trust in the sender or other things. What does the man's comment in Mark 1:40, "If you are willing…" tell you about the man's beliefs? Can you think of other misconceptions? Think about a situation that you cannot change – which of the various disguises do you hold on to?**

---

[13] Warren W. Wiersbe, *Be Holy*, (Col. Springs: Chariot Victor 1994)

5. One lesson we can learn from leprosy is that there is value in pain. Dr. Paul Brand worked with lepers for years. He said that greatest gift he could give to his patients was the gift of pain. God sometimes uses the pain of circumstances to get our attention. Is there some area in your life where God is trying to get your attention?

6. In Lev. 13 and 14 we learn that those with leprosy were considered unclean and had to be isolated from society because anyone who was touched by a leper was himself considered unclean. Review the paragraph below and comment on the lengths to which God will go to show His love for us.

Some scholars speculate that the reason Jesus told the healed leper to say nothing (Mark 1:43) was because if the man told people Jesus cleansed him, the curse of uncleanness would be on Jesus for seven days and He would be unable to enter a town or synagogue during that time. This is perhaps why Mark 1:45 indicates that Jesus stayed in unpopulated areas for several days. Think of the profoundness of this possibility! Here is a foreshadowing of the Cross. If Jesus indeed took on this leper's uncleanness, He bore the quarantine and rejection instead of the leper and took the leper's curse upon Himself. The leper went free, moving about the town telling people what had happened. Jesus is always consistently living out His true purpose.

As the study of Mark proceeds we will continue to learn more about the disciples and their problems, personalities, gifts and talents. We all have them – problems, personalities, gifts and talents. This week be thinking about the following:

> **Jesus told the leper not to tell anyone, and he told everyone; He tells us to tell everyone and we tell no one.**

- Ask God to show you WHAT He can use in your life to build His kingdom whether it be your gifts, talents, problems, pain.

- Ask God WHO are the people in your life who need Him? Consider co-workers, neighbors, sports moms, teachers, extended family.

- Ask God to create opportunities to deepen relationships with whomever He calls to mind.

- Find out WHEN – ask God to help you listen with His ears to these people so that you can hear their concerns, needs, problems.

- Find out HOW – ask God to show you what you can do to be His hands, feet, ears, voice in the lives of those people in your world. Record here what, if anything you heard and learned through the lessons in Chapter 1.

7. **Review this week's lesson and jot down one or two concepts or principles that you think would help you as you live your life as a member of the kingdom.**

Family Matters

I will be recommending several movies in the weeks to come, movies that relate to some part of the current week's lesson, as the following suggestion:

- *Molokai: The Story of Father Damien* – a true story about a 19th century priest, Father Damien, who risked everything to help people no one else would touch, the lepers of Molokai, Hawaii. When he saw the primitive conditions under which the island's lepers were forced to live, the shocked Damien went on a personal crusade to improve their physical and spiritual lives.

Looking Forward to Chapter 2

Who are your stretcher-bearers? Church is for the sick!

Chapter 2
Observing the Master in the Context of Conflict (Mark 2-3)

Day 1
Calls in the Midst of Conflict (Mark 2:1-17)

Background Information

In this lesson we see six different instances where Jesus and His call intersected with the religious leaders of the day. In order to understand the conflict and the depth of enmity that existed between them, it will help to understand who the religious leaders were.

Pharisees were called the separated ones. This group arose as an objection to the Jewish culture being watered down after the Maccabean revolt. Pharisees were mostly middle class laymen. While they did not appear to have a heart for the truth, they did have a healthy respect for the Law and strict obedience to it. They carefully followed Mosaic Law (The Torah) as well as the laws of the rabbis which grew out of Mosaic law (The Talmud). Many followed the laws to ridiculous lengths, but because of this they also gained respect from the masses for their devotion to the law.

For example, some rabbis believed spitting on the ground during Sabbath to be work because if the spit disturbed the dirt in any way, it could be considered plowing. Here's one some of us can relate to: a woman was not supposed to look in the mirror on the Sabbath because she might see a gray hair and be tempted to pluck it out, thus working on the Sabbath! Even the question of whether a Pharisee could eat an egg on the Sabbath was at issue – the unrepentant hen might have laid that egg on the Sabbath![14]

Scribes were not religious or political. They were the professionals: the lawyers, scribes and teachers of the law. Some were rabbis. They *interpreted* and taught the law (much like the judicial system today is meant to function). They made judicial decisions in cases brought to them; they interpreted questions such as, "What constitutes 'work' on the Sabbath?" In Jesus' day, most of the scribes were members of the Pharisees, though not all Pharisees were scribes. Jesus was considered one of them, a scribe. Thus His actions were often offensive because His interpretation differed so drastically from the religious leaders of the day.

The **Sadducees** controlled the priesthood. They were the educated, wealthy, prominent upper class citizens. A small select group, they believed ONLY in the Torah (first five books of the Old Testament) as authoritative. They denied oral laws of the non-priestly rabbis, didn't believe in angels, spirits or immortality of

---

[14] Robert H. Gundry, *Survey of the New Testament*, (Grand Rapids: Zondervan, 1970).

the soul. Nor did they believe in the resurrection of the body. As one wag put it, because they had no hope of resurrection they were *sad, you see*. Sadducees wanted the *status quo*; they didn't like re-interpreting the law to new circumstances in daily life. Their group was largely wiped out in AD 70 when the temple was destroyed.

Disciples' Perspective

In many ways Jesus was a revolutionary. He came to fulfill the law but in such a way that no one steeped in tradition or legalism could ever have imagined or even approved. He proposed to inform the mind, stir the heart and convert the will. He wanted to access men's inner lives to build on a deepening inner faith but not through force.

For the same reasons legislating morality today doesn't work, Jesus knew that teaching people to outwardly obey the laws without inwardly changing their hearts was a hopeless task. Jesus sought not to force people's wills but to change their hearts one by one which is still the mission today.

Historical Quote

"If you find the perfect church, they don't want you."

-Robert T. Seelye, one of my mentors

Getting to the Heart of the Matter

Today's Reading Mark 2:1-17
Parallel Passages: Matt. 9:1-13, Luke 5:17-32

I like Sue Thompson's modern day definition of Pharisee from her book, *The Prodigal Brother*[15]. She says a Pharisee is, "…a self righteous, pompous man or woman who presumes to speak for God and the establishment, who sees himself or herself as better than others, annoyed with those who aren't enlightened or as holy, irritated with anyone who seeks to change the status quo." This is sometimes a little too close to home for me. In the privacy of my own journalistic writings I have at times described myself as, "Me, the Pharisee!" How do you measure up?

1. **Read Mark 2:1-12. Make a list of persons/groups present.**

This portion of Scripture has become known to many as the stretcher bearer story. There is always a way to bring people to Jesus. Some people are creative and think way outside the box, as seen in this story. It is clear from the reading that the paralytic could not be healed without help from his friends. I have found in my own life that sometimes I am the stretcher bearer for others and, more often, I am the one on the stretcher counting on friends to bring me before Jesus.

---

[15] Sue Thompson, *The Prodigal Brother*, (Wheaton: Tyndale House, 2005).

The Call to Follow Jesus

2. How does the paralytic man get to Jesus? (Mark 2:3-5)

3. Faith that does the unexpected always gets God's attention. Whose faith was responsible for the paralytic's healing? What parallels can you draw from this story that will help you live out your life as Christ's disciple? (Mark 2:3-5)

4. Who are your stretcher bearers? Who can you call on in times of need in your own life?

5. Read Mark 2:6-8. What were the scribes' main complaint in this story? (Read Isa. 43:25 for a clue)

6. How did Jesus respond to the unseen state of the scribes' hearts? (Mark 2:8-11)

> The paralytic obviously believed that what God ordered him to do, He empowered him to do because the man got up and walked. Every time we receive a new assignment, whether it be to get up and walk, go out and start a ministry, or write a note to a sick friend, we are following in the footsteps of this man.

7. Besides the man himself, who benefitted from Jesus' healing of the man? (Mark 2:12-13)

Jesus moves things up a notch in this story by forgiving the paralytic's sins which only God has authority to do. (Isa. 43:25) This was not lost on the scribes present who were internally outraged by this show of authority. However, Jesus did not just come to be a great healer of physical pain and suffering – had that been His mission, neither you nor I would have any hope. He came for a much deeper purpose – to heal and make whole everyone who would come. Jesus knew it was more difficult to forgive sin than to heal. Seeking forgiveness for us sent Him to the Cross.

8. In the passage contrast the people's response to what occurred with the scribes' response. What are some reasons why people respond to facts differently? (Given the same set of facts, five people will respond in five different ways.)

9. How can you use what you discovered about people here as you live out your own life for Christ?

The Call of Levi, Mark 2:13-17

God eating with sinners! His extending friendship to them demonstrated the availability of God to all! This story also shows God's willingness to forgive anyone who would join Him. God is ever willing to forgive and engage. He would choose to eat with you or me for, "they are we."

To a Pharisee, the term *sinner* was one who refused to subject himself to the pharisaical interpretation of the law and follow all of the hundreds of laws they themselves put in place. According to that definition, Jesus would be considered a sinner since He did not follow every single law that the Pharisees and scribes put on the people.

10. **Read Mark 2:13-17. Make a list of who was present in this story.**

11. **Who was Levi? (Mark 2:14)**

12. **What was the main complaint of the Pharisees in this section? (Mark 2:16-17)**

> Tax collectors were selected based on their profit margin bids. The one with the lowest bid got the job, but would then illegally add to the tax amount to line their own pockets.

Whenever you are asked to state the complaint of the Pharisee, this should be a marker for you to check your own life. What Pharisaical complaints are you making in your own life? I only ask this of you because I constantly have to be on guard against my own complaining tendencies. If we put these under submission to Him immediately, we're less likely to exhibit other unhappy traits.

13. **What did Levi give up and what did he gain in order to follow Jesus? What lessons can we take from his choices for our lives today?**

14. **Jesus essentially told the Pharisees that God came to heal the sick, meaning that He came to make sinners whole. How does this story illustrate that principle?**

15. **Think of this principle in terms of church today. As a response to the statement, *The church is full of hypocrites*, how could you use Jesus' answer to the Pharisees to turn people's thinking around?**

Just this morning I saw on the internet a YouTube that went viral about a young man whose message essentially was, "I love Jesus, but I hate the church." It had over 18 million viewers and 313,000 likes! I also have acquaintances who feel the same way. I find it very sad in so many ways. We were meant for community with other believers; we were meant to gather together to worship and serve.

When asked why I go to church I tell people, "Church is for the sick and I am sick. I need to be where I can be touched and made whole, and sometimes I need the critiques that come out of other's mouths." We *are* the church. Having worked in a church I saw a lot of warts (some of them were mine), a lot of pain, many things that could have been done differently, but I also saw the love of Christ shine in that community. I saw people serving with no expectation of return, giving sacrificially, quietly meeting needs with no one even knowing. I saw a staff that prayed fervently and tried hard to bring quality programs to grow people, and I saw a pastor who never missed a death bed visit, even if the person wasn't of his congregation. That's hard to beat in this world!

I often use the parable of the BBQ briquette – when you pile a bunch together and light them, they stay hot for quite a long time. But what happens when one rolls away? It cools off and is no longer useful for its purpose. Do you see the parallel?

C.S. Lewis didn't like the church either but listen to his comment: He said when he became a believer he intended to do church on his own by retiring to his rooms and reading theology. He later found that was insufficient so he went to church where he disliked the hymns which he considered to be poorly written and composed. He explained that his conceit began to dissolve as he saw so many different people worshiping. "I realized that the hymns...were nevertheless being sung with devotion and benefit by an old saint in elastic side boots in the opposite pew, and then you realize you aren't fit to clean those boots. It gets you out of your solitary conceit."[16]

You may be one who struggles with the worthwhile-ness of the church. If so, I encourage you to pray diligently over this issue and talk it over with trusted believers or a growing pastor, making a prayerful decision, one that comes from the depth of kingdom living.

Day 2
Teaching in the Midst of Conflict (Mark 2:18-28)

Background Information

In this section Jesus told a story or parable about something well known in the culture of His day – putting new wine into old wineskins. Everyone understood the consequence. New goat skins filled with new fermenting wine stretches then

---

[16] C.S. Lewis, *God in the Dock*, (Grand Rapids: William B. Eerdmans 1970), 61-2.

dries and cracks, making it inflexible and unable to stretch with new wine again (not unlike some of us old bags who insist, "we've never done it that way!"). The old bags cannot contain the new kingdom lessons Jesus was coming to pour into all vessels willing to be made new.

His coming was not an appendage to Judaism nor was it a replacement of it. By giving us the parable of the wineskins, Jesus was comparing the old (the Law, total obedience to the Law and rigid formalism) with the new which would be a soul-life, Spirit-life relationship, not religion or a set of rules.

He also took on some of the establishment taboos – such as eating on the Sabbath and fasting. By His actions, He showed that religious practices are there to serve an actual spiritual purpose and to help us grow deeper in our walk with God. He did not nullify them or ignore them, but was trying to show that they are not to aid those who engage in them to become visible representations of the spiritual life. Nor are they given to us to make us feel righteous or even as a penance for wrongdoing. They are to aid us in our growth and search for a deeper relationship with Jesus.

Disciples' Perspective

So far this week we've learned something about the Pharisees, Sadducees and scribes who followed Jesus around not for what He could do for them, but out of curiosity as to how Jesus was attracting such large crowds and in hopes of catching Him in traps set for Him so that they might kill Him. (Mark 3:6) It didn't take religious leaders of the day long to realize that Jesus' teachings were not always in alignment with their own.

About now I'm wondering how the disciples were taking all of this in. They were present, but not much is said about them. Certainly they were seeing Jesus in a new light, as One having authority and who was not afraid to take on the problems of the day and the things that were keeping people in bondage. It might have been a good time for any disciple who couldn't stomach conflict to move on to another rabbi. Made of sterner stuff, of those selected to this point, all stayed with Jesus.

Historical Quote

"Have courage for the great sorrows of life and patience for the small ones; and when you have laboriously accomplished your daily task, go to sleep in peace. God is awake." -Victor Hugo

Getting to the Heart of the Matter

Today's Reading: Mark 2:18-28
Parallel passages: Matt. 9:14-17; Matt. 12:1-8; Luke 5:33-39; Luke 6:1-5

The Parable of the New Wineskins, Mark 2:18-22

In many ways, this parable is the key to Jesus' ministry. It tells us that adding Jesus to a life already full, but broken will never work. Only a new life can contain a new wine. It will never work to patch up the old life with new sayings and ideas. To put it another way, the old bags cannot contain Jesus. Make way for a new life!

1. **Read Mark 2:18-22. Make a list of who was present in this story.**

2. **What do you think Jesus was telling the Pharisees in Mark 2:18-20? Is there likewise a message to the disciples hidden here?**

3. **What happened to old wineskins when patches were sewn on to be used again? (Mark 2:21-22) Rewrite this passage in your own words to help you understand what an old wineskin filled with new wine might look like or how it could be used, if it could.**

> We must always be about our Father's business. If we fast, the purpose is not to be more righteous, but to be empowered to hear better, to serve better.

4. **Luke 5:36-39 tells us this passage is a parable, or story, to illustrate a particular point. What point do you think Jesus was trying to explain and who do you think the points were addressed to (disciples, Pharisees, or both)?**

Eating Grain on the Sabbath (Mark 2:23-28)

5. **Make a list of who was present in this story.**

6. **Look up Exodus 34:21. What is the real complaint of the Pharisees here?**

Jesus wasn't in a war with the individual Pharisees but with their belief system and how it burdened people and kept them down. *No one could ever be good enough* was the lie that Jesus came to free people from. By telling the people and the Pharisees that the "kingdom of heaven is at hand", He was telling them that it is right in front of you. In other words, "Here I am. I am the embodiment of the kingdom. Reach out and receive Me to find true freedom and hope." The same message is ours today.

7. **What do you think is the main principle Jesus was teaching His disciples in this story?**

8. **How do the principle(s) you came up with fit in today's society/culture?**

9. Review the four stories told in Mark 2 (Stretcher bearer story, Mark 2:1-12); (Levi's call, Mark 2:13-17); (wineskins, Mark 2:18-28); (Eating on the Sabbath, Mark 2:23-28). Look at the following principles below and decide which of the four stories they relate to:

(a) God loves me right now – just the way I am. I don't have to clean up my act before coming to Him.

(b) Jesus looks not for old bags, but for people who desire to grow and be open to whatever fresh gift God wants to pour into them.

(c) Jesus goes where people want wholeness.

(d) Sometimes I must carry people by my faith and other times, they must carry me.

(e) Religion is man's way of reaching God; Jesus is God's way of reaching man.

(f) The evidence of new life is joy.

(g) Only a new life can contain a new wine. You can't patch up the old life with new sayings and new ideas!

(h) To accept Jesus as Lord and Savior is to begin again – to reorient mind and heart around obedience to Him.

10. Which of the above principles do you find the most challenging in your life right now?

Day 3
The Call to Follow Jesus (Mark 3:1-20)

Background Information

The early Christians, especially in Rome, undoubtedly had an interest in how the church was actually formed. Mark, in his account in Chapter 3 tells us how the disciples were called and became apostles. This signifies the beginning of the infant church. You will also see in this chapter how the crowds continued to press upon Jesus for healing.

I was recently invited to attend a wine pressing at a local winery. Some friends had purchased an interest in a vat of wine. When I arrived, I saw a huge, silver juicer. It did rather look like my juicer, but much bigger. I was warned to stand back as the grapes were fed into the juicer since the force of the press made the juice from the grapes explode outward. Sure enough, though most of the juice went into the vat, some splattered the area around the juicer.

In this portion of Scripture, the word for pressing is the same word used to describe how grapes are pressed to extract juices. I understand the meaning of pressing much better having seen that demonstration. Mark uses this word several times to describe the depth of human need that was pressing in on Jesus. Some scholars believe that this factor led Jesus to realize that, while resident in His human body, He could not touch every need alone and that He needed to reproduce Himself to meet more needs. This in turn may have led Him to pray through the night (Luke 6:12) thus finding the wisdom to choose the twelve disciples, eleven who later became apostles.

In His humanness, He realized His own physical limitations in being able to be in only one place at any given moment. By training the twelve, His ability to be in more than one place at a time would be multiplied by a factor of twelve. This was a foreshadowing of when the Holy Spirit later came in Acts 1 whereby Jesus' power and the multiplication factor became magnified a thousand times a thousand and beyond.

Also in today's reading we see Jesus moving one step closer to the Cross as His love and compassion for hurting humanity prompts Him to heal a man in a synagogue on the Sabbath. This act of compassion sets the Scribes and Pharisees on a mission to see Him killed.

Disciples' Perspective

The qualifications of the twelve lead us to the inescapable conclusion that Jesus can use anyone willing to be led by Him. These men were not considered *prominent* or *important* in the synagogue, but they were willing learners. That being said, they were impulsive, temperamental, easily offended and had all the prejudices common to their day and ours too. If that sounds familiar to you, welcome to the world of the called of Christ!

Historical Quote

"When I vacillated about my decision to serve the Lord my God, it was I who willed and I who willed not, and nobody else. I was fighting against myself. All You asked was that I cease to want what I willed and want what You willed."

-St. Augustine

Getting to the Heart of the Matter

Scholars almost universally believe that in choosing twelve men to follow Him, Jesus was thinking of the twelve tribes of Israel whom God originally planned to impart the message of salvation. Twelve is the number of new government or new administration. Something new is on the horizon and the disciples are in on the ground floor.

Today's Reading: Mark 3:1-20
Parallel Passages: Matt. 12:9-14; Luke 6:6-16

1. **Read Mark 3:1-6. Make a list of who is present.**

2. **What did Jesus do in this section (Mark 3:1-4)? Why do you think He was angry and grieved? (Mark 3:5)**

3. **Isn't it ironic that it was on the Sabbath that the Scribes determined in their hearts to kill Jesus? (Mark 3:6) What does this say about outward obedience to the law without inward change in the heart?**

4. **Read Mark 3:7-12. Make a list of who is present.**

5. **In Mark 3:10 the crowd pressed in on Jesus in order to touch Him. Do you think Jesus ever felt discouraged that people weren't as interested in Him for His message as they were for what He could do for them? Do you ever feel 'pressed upon' in your own life? Write an example.**

6. **What happened to the unclean spirits when they saw Jesus? (Mark 3:11-12) How do you think they recognized Him?**

7. **Read Mark 3:13-19. Also read Luke 6:12-16. According to Luke, what did Jesus do before He chose the twelve? What practical applications can you make from this?**

8. **Read Mark 3:14-15 carefully. What tasks did Jesus appoint to the twelve?**

9. **What is the message here for those who are His disciples, whether it be the twelve, or you and me?**

10. **Read 1 Cor. 1:26-31. What does Paul tell us about how God calls men and women to be His instruments of peace, healing and cover for a desperate world? Make a list of the characteristics listed.**

11. **In Mark 3:14-15 note the progression of the calling starting with appointment, companionship, commission and authority. Write your thoughts about the significance of the progression in terms of discipleship today or you on your own journey.**

12. **Read John 15:16. Who does the choosing?**

13. **Note from the passage in Mark and Luke the names that are given to the various disciples. Some are given new names (such as Peter). Why do you think Jesus gave them different names?**

14. **The word for *authority* in Mark 3:15 is the word meaning *delegated authority*. It is not something from within yourself, but something delegated to you from God. You are the hands, He is the healer; you are the voice, He is the one who calls and draws people. What do these ideas communicate to you?**

Recently I came across a section in my journal where I interacted with Mark 3:11-12. It contains a different perspective on seeing that might assist you in your kingdom journey. I close today's lesson with this thought from my April 2011 journal: "Mark 3:11-12 has an interesting encounter between Jesus and 'evil spirits'. Crowds were coming to Him for healing. Scripture records, "And when those possessed by evil spirits *caught sight of Him*, the spirits would throw them [people] to the ground in front of Him shrieking, 'You are the Son of God.'" The kind of spiritual power that was emanating from Jesus was undoubtedly amazing. Were there any spiritual people besides those who were possessed who could truly *see* Him? I think of Simeon when Jesus was a baby, and Anna. I suspect some who believed they could be healed saw something in Him. The woman with the issue of blood comes to mind. But was there anyone besides these who recognized Him instantly in their spirit? Would I have done so? Or even more, would those with evil spirits recognize the Spirit in me? Do I live in His power such that others can see? I remember one of the Catholic ladies at my dad's nursing home one time, when I bent down to her wheelchair to say hello, said to me, "I see God in you." I got tears in my eyes. What did she see? How did she know? I want more of Jesus."

Day 4
The Pincer Maneuver (Mark 3:20-30)

Background Information

In this section of Scripture Jesus confronts and is confronted. I do not have a military background but I am a student of history and love well-done war movies and books. I've learned a few things over the years – like the *pincer maneuver* which, according to Wikipedia (Wikipedia n.d.), allows "the enemy to attack the center, sometimes in a charge, then attacking the flanks of the charge." We see this in today's reading when Jesus, pressed in on by the crowd from the center is also *pinched* by both sides – the scribes on the one hand and His own family[17] on the other.

This is everyday life in the raw – something we all experience. We often know who our detractors are, such as in the case where Jesus knew the scribes and Pharisees were out to get Him. But occasionally unexpected things occur which take us completely by surprise. Here, Jesus' family showed up to take Him home thinking He has gone mad. It is entirely possible that Satan was behind both flank attacks on Jesus. If the Scribes were unsuccessful in turning the crowds, perhaps Jesus could be persuaded by His family to be moved out of the public eye. It could have ended right there and the rest of the story might not have been told.

We must understand (and not blame) that even well meaning, loving family and friends can sometimes be tools in the hands of the enemy to pull you and me away from our true calling and purpose.

Years ago, I experienced a flank attack by another leader in our church who went to the senior pastor to complain about a decision I had made. Had I been my usual confrontive self, I might have missed the opportunity to be an encourager to this person. In this one instance, the Holy Spirit prodded me to pray and listen and not run to the pastor with my side of the story. As I did so, I understood two things: (1) The person who had complained about me was also in pain, feeling

Beelzebub, meaning "Lord of the Flies", was considered by the Jews to be the supreme demon among evil spirits. He could also be called Satan.

---

[17] The actual meaning could refer to "friends", "relatives" or "those on His side", not just family. For a more thorough discussion of this issue, refer to William Hendriksen, *The New Testament Commentary: The Gospel of Mark,* (Grand Rapids: Baker Book House, 1975), 132.

The Call to Follow Jesus

overlooked and had felt misunderstood for years; (2) sometimes even people who deeply love Jesus (like me and you and this other person) can be unwitting tools in the enemy's hand to thwart and deflect the calling on someone else's life. Not so Jesus. As you read the passage for today, watch how He counters both attacks.

Disciples' Perspective

The disciples were present during these confrontations Jesus faced. (See Mark 3:20) They had just been called by Jesus up to the mountain and were commissioned by Him having been given authority in Jesus' Name to be sent out to share the words they received. Coming down from the mountain energized, excited and ready to serve, they walked into a situation where they didn't even have time to eat. For the first time they saw what they themselves might be up against if they continued to follow Jesus. It is much the same way we might feel after hearing a great sermon, being encouraged at a weekend conference or a retreat and then hitting Monday morning reality.

Historical Quote

Thomas Brooks, 17th century Puritan pastor wrote, "Satan promises the best but pays with the worst; he promises honor and pays with disgrace; he promises pleasure and pays with pain; he promises profit and pays with loss; he promises life and pays with death."

Getting to the Heart of the Matter

Today's Reading: Mark 3:20-30
Parallel Passages: Matt. 12:22-45; Luke 11:14-26

1. **From your reading of Chapter 2, what do you think prompted Jesus' family to such a drastic action in Mark 3:21?**

2. **Let's evaluate the thinking process of the scribes in Mark 3:22 and 30. Write down the three things they are saying about Jesus and state what they are accusing Him of doing.**

Actually, the scribes were correct in thinking that Jesus' power was supernatural but their conclusions about how He came by it were tragically wrong. Even then the truth was twisted to suit the purpose to minimize Jesus' authority and power.

3. **Can you think about some examples of how this same thinking shows up today in how people sometimes come up with the right conclusion for the wrong reasons.**

Speaking of the right conclusion for the wrong reasons, you can use this method to teach your children when watching nature and history specials on TV. Several years ago we were watching a series on mysteries of the Bible. The commentator in discussing archaeological findings, indicated that in many ancient locales of the Holy Land, idols were found in Jewish homes. This was a true statement but the conclusion reached was wrong. The commentator concluded that the early Jews therefore were not mono-theistic (believing in One God) but were poly-theistic (believing in many gods).

Actually, the truth is that the Jews *were* a mono-theistic people, but they were living in sin and idolatry. As the Scripture explains over and over, people often fell into sin and worshipped idols in their homes and their holy places, causing them to go into captivity. (Not unlike you and me today.)[18]

We used this opportunity to discuss with our son the importance of being able to think critically and compare the truth (as found in Scripture) with the evidence. The commentator's facts were correct, but his *opinion/conclusion* was erroneous. We must learn to watch for opinion masked as conclusion or truth. Everything must be evaluated through the lens/truth of Scripture.

4. **Write out the four statements made by Jesus in response to the scribes' accusations in Mark 3:23-26. Try to summarize His message in one sentence.**

5. **Mark 3:27 is an important verse in that it teaches much about the strategy of Satan, the enemy of our souls, and how Jesus effects our rescue from his territory. In this verse, Jesus tells us five important facts about the enemy and our rescue. Review the verse and see how many things you can come up with, then review the text box below on Mark 3:27.**

6. **Only one who is stronger than Satan can enter his realm and bind him as was done here. The expulsion of demons is nothing less than a forceful attack on the power of Satan. Jesus' ability to cast out demons shows that one stronger than Satan has come to restrain his activity and release the captives. What areas do you perceive in your own life to be strongholds from which you need release? Commit to pray over them.**

---

[18] For a detailed study on this topic, watch for my upcoming study on *Idols in My Pocket: Selected Studies in Kings.*

> Mark 3:27 says no one can enter (or bring about a rescue) the *strong man's house* (Satan's domain) and *plunder* (steal or take the goods by force) his *property* (the souls of men and women caught in his traps) UNLESS he first *binds* the strong man (makes the strong man's power ineffective or neutral) and then he will *plunder his house*. Jesus came to bind the strong man and He did so through the Cross. It was the only way to free the captives. (See Isaiah 61:1-4; Luke 4:14-21.)

Mark 3:28-30 discusses the *unforgiveable sin*. Scholars don't really know what the unforgiveable sin is, but most seem to agree that it is not something God does but is something we do. The most popular and likely meaning is that the unforgiveable sin is not God's refusal to forgive, but man's refusal to accept His free gift.

7. **Do you think any of us can even know whether someone has finally committed this particular sin? If so, when do you give up praying for that person, if ever?**

Our family motto comes from the movie, *Galaxy Quest*: "Never give up! Never surrender!" Had I not taken that motto on, I might never have seen my brother come to faith in Christ. He spent nearly a lifetime running from God, but God is faithful and never gives up calling on people when we pray for them.

Were you as riveted as I was by the translation of Mark 3:27? My life has been changed by the Lord's exposure of strongholds in me and as I have studied, taught and written how the enemy takes us captive, I have been able to look at this whole area in a new way. Recognizing my own hidden captivity, even as a believer for many years was quite revealing and transforming. The Lord has freed me from some strongholds that prevented me from pursuing writing and several other areas as well. He has brought about breakthrough and continues to do so in my life (and there are a lot more!) It is what He desires for all of us.

Having reviewed verses like Mark 3:27, Isaiah 61:1-4 and Luke 4:14-21, hopefully God has begun to move in your life too. It wasn't only the disciples who could not see – sometimes it is you and me. Sometimes we are so in bondage that we aren't even aware of it and it holds us back from walking more deeply into His presence. Jesus said that He came that we might live an abundant life. (John 10:10) It took me years to figure it out and I'm still learning.

Day 5
Jesus' Family Matters (Mark 3:31-35)

Background Information

At first glance Mark 3:31-35 appears very troubling and might seem like Jesus is rejecting His own family. Mark however, is writing to the church at Rome which had a desperate need for a sense of community and encouragement. What Jesus was really saying is that kinship with Him is determined not by family ties, but by "whosoever comes." Remember too, that His family eventually did come to trust and believe in Him. His half-brother James was the head of the church in Jerusalem (Acts 15:13-23) and is believed to have written the Book of James. He came to believe so solidly that he was martyred for his faith.

As Hendriksen points out after a thorough analysis of this section of Scripture, "We just don't know" what it means. But as history records and Hendriksen further reports, Jesus was not the only one to suffer misunderstandings due to His actions. The Apostle Paul was likewise accused of, "being out of his mind." (Acts 26:24); Martin Luther's detractors claimed he was of the devil; Francis Assisi was called, 'the mad son of Bernadone'[19] as well as many others throughout history. Jesus was the cornerstone and the first of thousands upon thousands who would follow Him, taking on any slur or any name just for the privilege of serving and suffering for Him.

Disciples' Perspective

The disciples were learning that Jesus never wasted an interruption. As the message of Jesus' waiting family rippled through the crowd in this story, He turned the interruption into a teachable moment by opening up the minds of His hearers to describe the community of the new wineskins as being like a family in form. This greatly encouraged the Roman believers for whom Mark wrote to stand firm and recognize they were not alone in the midst of the persecution which surrounded them.

Historical Quote

"Jesus often let other people's interruptions determine His daily schedule."
- Philip Yancey[20]

Getting to the Heart of the Matter

Today's Reading: Mark 3:31-35
Parallel passages: Matt. 12:46-50; Luke 8:19-21

---

[19] Hendriksen, IBID. at 134.
[20] Philip Yancey, *Rumors of Another World*, (Grand Rapids: Zondervan, 2003).

1. Why do you think Jesus' mother and brothers were standing outside and not in? (Mark 3:31; see also Mark 3:20-21)

2. Look at the Historical Quote above. When was the last time God interrupted your day?

3. Think about any flank attacks you might have encountered recently and write them down here. Were you aware at the time what was happening? What did you learn from it?

Jesus was in a difficult spot in having to decide to choose between family and obedience to God's will. Just read anyone's story of conversion from Islam to Christianity and you will get a taste of Jesus' dilemma that day.

After reading Mark 3:31-35, consider what Jesus was really saying. Was he speaking to the church, do you think? If so, what does the church represent to you today? Is it more like a spiritual supermarket where you go, get what you need and leave, or is it a family brought together for a common purpose.

4. What needs to change in your attitude or life to live in conformity with what Jesus said to His hearers?

5. How is a family like a church?

6. Review this week's lesson and jot down one or two concepts or principles that you think would help you as you live your life as a member of the kingdom.

To choose between His Father's will (to preach the kingdom) and His family's call (to remove Him from the public eye and carry the stigma of mad man) could not have been an easy road. Thankfully for us, He will always choose the harder path. The enemy used every possible snare to distract Jesus from His purpose. Perhaps you have had a similar experience.

Family Matters

This week I have two movies to recommend:

- *Facing the Giants* -- one great movie that shows how a group of young men, not unlike the twelve disciples, were chosen and trained for a common purpose.

- *More Than Dreams* -- a remarkable series of five short stories told in their original language (but well worth reading sub-titles) to really help us to understand the price some people pay to follow Jesus. It is one of the best movies I have ever seen. (Available at http://morethandreams.org).

Looking Forward

In the next chapter, we will focus on the ministry of multiplication and how Jesus did it.

Chapter 3
The Call to Follow Jesus (Mark 4-5)

Day 1
Stories from Heaven (Mark 4:1-20)

Background Information

Everybody loves a good story! One of my closest friends, Linda, is one of the best story-tellers I have ever heard. When she tells a story, even if it's one I've heard before, I am on the edge of my seat waiting for the punch line. As a Director of Children's Ministry she understands the value of story-telling to make an important spiritual point.

Jesus was the greatest story-teller. When He told stories, even if people thought they knew what was coming, they were always astonished at His teaching because He made the old, new; He gave the story life; His stories freed people from bondage. He told them kingdom stories which other rabbis of the day were not able to tell since they were not experiencing kingdom living. And even if the people didn't understand all of what they heard, they were still astonished and went away full. Sometimes, as we will see, experiencing fullness in kingdom living takes time. Some lessons take years to understand and grasp.

In this week's lesson Jesus spoke in parables. Hendriksen in his study of Mark defines a parable as, "An earthly story with a heavenly meaning."[21] In the original language, the word *parable* has the same interest-promoting effect on its hearers as, "Once upon a time," in our day.

To many hearers, Jesus' parables while fascinating, were obscure with their meanings hidden. This was actually part of Jesus' strategy. As training of the twelve continued, Jesus used parables as a method of sifting the wheat from the chaff. "He who has an ear, let him hear," was often spoken by Jesus.

It is important to note for future studies *why* Jesus used parables. He spoke in parables to instruct His disciples but to conceal His teaching from superficial, antagonistic hearers. His enemies were rejecting His teaching; the multitudes were there, not for Him, but for what He could give them and were largely indifferent to the truth of why He came. Parables were used to attract those who hungered and thirsted after righteousness.

---

[21] Hendriksen, IBID. 148.

To the hard-pressed church of Mark's day the four parables in this chapter emphasize the truth that disappointment and suffering are within God's hidden wisdom; that patient waiting will pay off; that supernatural power complements human effort; that gifts are given to be used and that the kingdom of God is indeed among them!

Later in this chapter, as we continue our journey into the Call, we will see that the disciples were getting not only an earful (Mark 4), but an eye-full as well. They saw the Power of God evident in Jesus' life as they witnessed His command over the elements (Mark 4:35-41), His authority over demons (Mark 5:1-20), His dominance over pain and suffering (Mark 5:25-34), and His supremacy over death (Mark 5:21-24 and :35-43).

From a man whose life was more of a living death (the Garasene demoniac) to a young girl whose spirit is restored (Jairus' daughter), Jesus changes people and faith grows. From a wild sea (4:37) to a wild man (5:3-5), Jesus' power was evident in every corner of life. Both were untamable without God's help.

Disciples' Perspective

From this point on in the gospel narrative Jesus mostly focused on the twelve disciples but He didn't isolate them from the masses. Their training proceeded in the midst of the multitude they were to serve. Jesus spoke to the masses and later explained His lessons in more detail to the disciples. Jesus was imparting secrets of the kingdom to those He was closest to because only He could see their future.

Through the parables Jesus was teaching them to absorb what they were seeing and hearing. He wanted them to know and understand that they were born to teach others to absorb the things of God so that the ones they taught in turn could teach others…and so it goes. He also wanted to teach them to understand that seeing God in the ordinary is an important concept for growth. Once again, their journey is our journey.

We were bought with a price and were not born for ourselves, but to learn, understand, observe, absorb and follow so that we too might become dispensers of Truth by using our life stories, gifts and talents for His glory.

Historical Quote

"Ice breaks many a branch, and so I see a great many persons bowed down and crushed by their afflictions. But now and then I meet one that sings in affliction, and then I thank God for my own sake as well as his…"
- -Henry Ward Beecher

Getting to the Heart of the Matter

Today's Reading: Mark 4:1-20
Parallel Passages: Matt. 13:1-23; Luke 8:14-18

The word for *listen* in this passage means, "Be listening; respond."

1. **Read today's passage and circle in your Bible the words: *listen, hear, ear*. What do you think Jesus is trying to tell His listeners by these words?**

2. **Write down what you think these symbols in the story stand for: The Sower; the Seed; the ground; the birds; the rocky soil, the thorns.**

3. **Define the following terms: (You might want to check out a dictionary)**

   (a) Mystery

   (b) Unresponsive

   (c) Impulsive

   (d) Preoccupied

4. **What do you think is the *mystery* in this section? (Mark 4:11)**

In this section, Jesus speaks to the masses in Mark 4:4-9 and then explains the parable to His disciples in Mark 4:10-20.

5. **Read Mark 4:4 and 4:15 together. These verses describe *the resistant or unresponsive heart*. These people do nothing with the message given and in some ways are resistant to it. How did Jesus describe the unresponsive heart?**

In the Palestine of Jesus' day paths were placed between the rows of planted crops for the farmer to walk on to move about the field. Travelers also used these paths. (Refer to Mark 2:23.) The paths were often hardened and packed down from foot traffic, which could offer an explanation for the hard soil mentioned in this parable.

The *Kingdom of God* is the powerful manifestation of the reign of the God's kingdom in the hearts and lives of His people. It is part of the mystery of belonging to Jesus. Remember, a kingdom implies a ruler and a rule. Who rules your heart today?

6. **Think of some reasons why people might be unresponsive to the Word. (Read Ezekiel 33:31-32 for some help.)**

Read Mark 4:5-6 and 4:16-17 together. This section describes the *impulsive heart*. (Note how many times the word *immediately* is used). These are spur-of-the-moment people who immediately accept what they hear and just as immediately reject it. They get caught or are ensnared by problems and afflictions and are done.

7. **How did Jesus describe the person with an *impulsive heart*?**

Read Mark 4:7 and 4:18-19 together. This section describes the *preoccupied* or *distracted heart*.

8. **What three things did Jesus say in Mark 4:19 fills their hearts? How do you see this manifest in people's lives today?**

9. **What things distract people from getting to know God?**

10. **As you think about Jesus' mission in Mark 1:14-15 (you may need to review it), what do you think the purpose of seed sowing is? How does the seed grow once it is heard and received?**

11. **Read Mark 4:8 and 4:20 together. How did Jesus describe this person's heart? What do you think the significance of the 30-60-100 fold increase refers to?**

12. **Armed with the meaning of parable ("earthly story with heavenly meaning"), describe an everyday event in your life that can be used to teach a heavenly message. (Hint: Almost every event in your life or your children's lives can be a parable if you are watching for God's meaning).**

Perhaps to your surprise you see yourself represented in one of these pictures above. If so, take heart and take hope. This is the Lord speaking to you. Jesus has gifted you with wisdom and discernment and is calling you to the deeper walk with Him.

As we close today's lesson, I want you to consider the four types of soils mentioned in today's parable. While most scholars teach the parable refers to four different types of people who hear the Word and how it impacts them as individuals, I would like you to think outside the box with me for just a moment. Consider yourself in the place of each of the four types of soil mentioned above. While most of you probably are hearers that have heard with great joy and received gladly the message given, I wonder if there are times in your life when maybe your heart represents one of the other types of soil mentioned in this story.

Speaking for myself, there are areas in my life where the enemy comes in and snatches the Word away before I can even dwell on it. I may *know* something but I let my own bondage and strongholds overtake my heart. I don't even realize it, but sometimes my answer to God's call is *no* before I am even fully aware of the question! (Mark 4:4) Other times in my life, I lack the depth and staying power to wait things out as I am often asked to do by the Lord. I try, but I let my complaints be made known to God and everyone else around me. (Mark 4:5)

There are other areas that I have difficulty in surrendering because I am so preoccupied with my own issues and the things going on around me. Sometimes I'm even "busy for Him," but still preoccupied. Probably some of you see yourself in this way as well. If so, would you consider the four areas from a personal standpoint, write one area you struggle with and pray over one area that seems to be relevant in your life today. As we will see in the next section, the more we give Him, the more we receive from Him.

Day 2
The Bigness of Small Beginnings (Mark 4:21-34)

Background Information

Stories from heaven continue in today's reading as we look at three more parables. Two of the three are farming related and are given to the disciples as addendums to the Parable of the Sower. They deal specifically with kingdom living. As you read Mark 4:26-29, keep in mind that Mark is the only one of the gospels to tell this parable.

In Chapter 1, we talked about the kingdom of heaven and the kingdom of God as being God's kingship and rule in us as we live-out our faith. In this section we will see two specific parables which describe the kingdom of heaven. Pay close attention as you read these parables to see what aspects of kingdom living you can gain from the stories.

Disciples' Perspective

Of the three short parables we will look at today, these stories were given directly to the disciples for their understanding. While Jesus still taught the masses, some truths were hidden (Mark 4:11-12) and meant only for true followers. It is not that Jesus did not want people to know, it was more that the *people themselves* didn't want to know. That is what we learned in yesterday's parable of the Sower.

The principle Jesus taught the disciples was to realize that their lives were not their own; that they had a responsibility to sow kingdom seeds even when it seemed like nothing was happening. *As they were obedient to the kingdom call*, the mere act of obedience increased their own ability to see, hear and absorb.

Historical Quote

"If the disciples deliver to the church that which they have received of the Lord, they shall be led more into the secrets of the Lord. Gifts and graces multiply by being exercised; and God has promised to bless the hand of the diligent."[22]
                                                                                    -Matthew Henry

> Those who are reluctant to share their faith may have too little of it or it may not have really grabbed their lives. Are you conserving your light or sharing it?

Getting to the Heart of the Matter

Today's Reading: Mark 4:21-34
Parallel Reading: Matt. 13:31-35; Luke 13:18-21

Parable of the Lamp stand (Mark 2:21-25)

1. **What does the lamp or candle represent in this parable? (See Psalm 119:105; Matthew 5:14).**

2. **Who has the power to hide the light of the candle?**

3. **Without spiritualizing the issue think about some sources of light and what light does. Where do you think the light comes from in this parable?**

---

[22] Matthew Henry, *Commentary on the Whole Bible, Vol. 5*, (n.p., n.d.).

The Call to Follow Jesus

4. **What do you think causes people to shine for Jesus? Give some examples.**

5. **What happens when we do not let our light shine?**

6. **How do you think the rabbis of the day were hiding the light of truth?**

7. **Read Mark 4:24-25. Summarize what the Scripture says to the disciples in these two verses. What does it mean for your life today?**

8. **Read Mark 4:26-29. What do these verses tell you about the kingdom of God?**

In the sower parable, the important thing is that the soil (our hearts) be right and ready. In this parable however, the farmer realized that once the seed has been cast he could do nothing more about it, but has to trust the mystery of the seed to do what it is supposed to do.

9. **Read Isa. 55:10-11. Who is responsible for the seed's bearing fruit?**

10. **Read Mark 4:30-34. What do these verses tell you about the kingdom of God?**

The mustard seed is the smallest seed in the garden (about the size of a pin-head) and can grow 10-12 feet tall. What seems small and insignificant to us may become great in God's plan.

11. **Lloyd J. Ogilvie says the mustard seed reflects, "the bigness of small beginnings."[23] What does this say about,**

    (a) Your own walk with Christ

---

[23] Ogilvie, IBID.

(b) The church today

(c) The disciples who were hearing Jesus tell this story?

One of my best friends, Karen, grows Monarch Butterflies in her yard. She provides a friendly environment, food for them to eat and a safe place to cocoon and mature into what they were meant to be. She understands too that they cannot be hurried in their hatching. As she watches them struggle to be free of the chrysalis that is holding them in, she realizes she must not help it to emerge. Even though it is desperately struggling, she understands that the struggling butterfly needs to go through the breaking free process on its own. To help it along out of compassion is to consign it to an early death.

Her understanding reminds me of the parable Jesus tells in Mark 4:26-29 where the seed is cast and must mysteriously germinate in the hearts of those who receive it. Some people struggle for years to emerge into the truth; others give up the struggle altogether, but, as the Scripture records, "the soil produces crops by itself." You and I cannot play the role of Holy Spirit in people's lives. He is the One who draws people to Himself. We are only the seed scatterers who occasionally get to water and bring in the harvest.

It is God alone Who knows what is happening in the dark chrysalis of people's lives as they struggle to find truth and gain freedom. Our job is to continue to scatter seeds and to pray for those who are seeking.

Day 3
Power Over Nature (Mark 4:35-41)

Background Information

A number of years ago a young pastor at our church gave a sermon and told a story about flying home on Super-Bowl Sunday. The pilot reported the ending score as the plane was landing. Because of the time difference, when the pastor got home the game was still on and his room-mates were in the throes of the game while he sat smugly smiling because he knew how the game was going to end. He used that story to tell a spiritual truth – that as believers we know the end of the story and can rest assured that it will come to pass.

In today's study the disciples were panicked in the storm. They had not heard or absorbed what they had supposedly learned that very day! So very much like the rest of us, don't you think? They were learning faith through their fear. Albert Barnett says, "Faith is the remedy for fear."[24] This is the first of four faith lessons that Jesus will give to His disciples in the rest of this chapter.

As Jesus and the disciples got into a boat near evening and went across the Sea of Galilee away from the crowds, it had already been a busy day and there was more to come. While Jesus was sleeping in the boat, Scripture records a "furious storm or hurricane" suddenly came up on the sea.[25] Even the seasoned fishermen in the boat were frightened by it, though scholars tell us that sudden storms were common in this area.

The Sea of Galilee is 13 miles long and 8 miles wide. It is in a depression or bowl surrounded by high hills or mountains. When cool air from the mountains sweep down into the narrow passage between the hills, it collides with the heated air above the lake sometimes causing violent winds to whip up the sea.[26] It must have been quite a terrifying storm as waves beat the boat and it began to fill up with water.

That Jesus was asleep in the midst of the melee gives us a flavor of what it was like to be "God in a body." Exhausted, limited, needing sleep, yet He could rest at such a time. It is a visual lesson on trusting. It shows His understanding that His Heavenly Father has it all under control.

Disciples' Perspective

Today's lesson is all about the disciples. They were beginning to move out of the curiosity stage and were becoming convinced that Jesus was in fact Who He said He was, though as we will see, it was more of a 'three steps forward, two steps back' lifestyle.

At the same time, their own lives were being changed forever. As a result, the whole world would never be the same. Jesus changes people one life at a time and His mandate to us and His disciples is to be a part of His work in doing the same.

Historical Quote

"There are no ordinary people...it is immortals who we joke with, work with, marry, snub and exploit. Immortal horrors or everlasting splendors...we should therefore, do all we can to nudge people toward Christlikeness."

-C.S. Lewis, *Weight of Glory.*

---

[24] Albert Barnett, *Disciples to Such a Lord*, (New York: Abingdon Press, 1957).
[25] Kenneth Wuest, *Wuest's Word Studies From the Greek New Testament, Vol. 1* (Grand Rapids: Wm. B. Eerdmans 1973), 96.
[26] Hendriksen, IBID.

Getting to the Heart of the Matter

Today's Reading: Mark 4:35-41
Parallel Passages: Matt. 8:23-27; Luke 8:22-25

Sometimes I feel like I'm the only one in the boat doing any rowing. It makes me feel cranky, annoyed and out-of-sorts. Is anyone with me on this? What's the remedy? Scripture tells us that fearless faith in the midst of the storm is the answer. Let's follow in Jesus' footsteps and go take a nap!

1. Review and summarize Jesus' and the disciples' day(s) so far beginning with Mark 2:1. What did they do during the day up to this point?

2. Read Mark 4:35-41 and report what *He* was doing and what *they* were doing.

3. Look at Mark 4:39. What two things did Jesus do?

4. What happened after Jesus spoke to the storm? Have you ever experienced the sensation of immediate calm in your own life after having come through a stormy trial?

5. Why do you think the disciples, some of whom were fishermen, called on Jesus the carpenter for help?

6. In Mark 4:38 what does the phrase, "Don't you care that we are perishing?" imply?

7. In Mark 4:40 Jesus asked the disciples, "Why *are* you afraid?" Not, "Why *were* you afraid?" What do you think He is really asking the disciples?

8. Read Mark 4:41. What does the awe of the disciples tell you about their growing understanding of Who Jesus is?

We've had the parable stories of Mark 4. In Mark 5 the disciples were heading into the live action living parables just like the 'living parable' you wrote about your own life earlier. They (and we) were about to start learning how story becomes application.

As you ponder this section of Scripture keep in mind that while it actually happened, it too is a parable. The boat in early church thinking symbolized the church. The waves symbolized the evil around them; the wind symbolized troubles, persecution, and affliction. Early Christian art often depicted Jesus standing calm in the middle of a boat. It must have been a great comfort to the suffering church at Rome to hear this story. What lessons do you think we can learn from this today?

Perhaps you have been in the boat while Jesus is apparently sleeping. Sometimes it seems that way as we go through the storms of life. But in His sleeping is the perfect picture of trust in His Heavenly Father. Even His sleeping can teach us something about trusting. As He calmed the sea and the wind with a word, Jesus gave this brief, unveiled moment to His disciples in the midst of their intense fear so that they could see Who He really is. Are you watching for Him to show up in your life? He unveils Himself to those who seek Him, sometimes in the most unexpected ways. He invites each of us to answer the question the disciples were asking, "Who is this Person that even the wind and the sea obey Him?"

Day 4
Power Over the Spirit World (Mark 5:1-20)

Background Information
In the last session we summarized Jesus and the disciples' day and it's not over yet! In this lesson the group crosses the Sea of Galilee on the same evening, encountering a furious storm, probably arriving in the middle of the night. Upon arrival they walked straight into the path of a wild man who accosted them as they were getting out of the boat.

This was possibly an unfamiliar area to the disciples. The area known as Decapolis (or 10 cities) was largely Gentile in population so the culture might have been different from the known Hebrew culture and it is likely that they didn't spend much time on this side of the sea.

Also, while demon possession was not unknown and in fact was fairly common in their time, the story Mark (and Luke) record is very graphic, giving much detail in how the poor man with the legion of demons survived. Juxtaposed alongside of his horrible living situation was Jesus who, with a word changed the man's life forever and, in doing so, sent the first missionary on his way, making not a few townspeople quite unhappy with how He did things.

Today we are going to look at this man's life in depth and encounter a subject that very few of us are comfortable with. Yet because Jesus addressed it and touched it, so must we. When studying a particular book of the Bible we should not ignore the uncomfortable parts or skip over the sections that don't match up with our own particular theology. Instead, we need to continue to seek truth because all Scripture is inspired by God and is profitable for our teaching. (2 Tim. 3:16-17) Learning to face the difficult areas will encourage us to pray for wisdom and instruction from the One Who guides us into all truth. (John 16:13)

The area of demon possession is not something to treat lightly. William Lane in his commentary on this section says, "Mark's account more graphically than any other in the gospels, indicates that the function of demonic possession is to destroy and particularly to destroy the image of God in men."[27]

We will be looking more into this subject as the weeks go on as Jesus taught the disciples more and more about the power and the lifestyle needed to confront this area. There are, however, many modern day questions that this study is not equipped to answer. For further study in this area ask your pastor or other respected believer for additional resources.

That being said, we won't be side-stepping issues either. We will look at where Jesus went, what He did and what the disciples were seeing, hearing and learning. And we will focus our attention on what we can learn directly from their encounters.

> **In modern Cairo nearly one million people live in cemeteries with houses literally built on tombs.**

Disciples' Perspective

We can only imagine the disciples' thoughts. Still shaken from the storm and the realization that they had amongst them One who could stop the wind and calm the sea, they were now facing a crazy man in the middle of the night. If it weren't so serious we could almost chuckle over their supposed reactions. *Good grief! What now? Doesn't anyone sleep around here? Is this how the Gentiles live? I thought so all along! We're all going to die! Will this day ever end?* We don't hear or see much of the disciples in this section of Scripture as they aren't mentioned, so we will need to look at this scenario from what Jesus wanted to teach them in the midst of it. As you have hopefully learned by now, "they are we." There are lessons to be caught and taught!

Historical Quote

British author G. K. Chesterton (1874 - 1936) was once asked, along with several other prominent citizens by the Times to write an essay on the subject, "What's

---

[27] Lane, IBID. 180.

Wrong with the World?" His essay is one of the finest, clearest and shortest essays ever written: "*Dear Sirs, I am. Sincerely yours, G. K. Chesterton.*"

Getting to the Heart of the Matter

Today's Reading: Mark 5:1-20
Parallel Passages: Luke 8:26-39, Matt. 8:28-34

We will look at these same verses from three different perspectives: The man, the demons and the townspeople.

Who is the Man?

Let's start today by doing a composite study of the demon-possessed man in Mark 5:1-20 (using parallel Scriptures from Luke 8:26-39). Answer the following questions:

1. **What clues do you find about his life before being taken over by demons?**

2. **Make a list of the personality characteristics of the man before Jesus came. (What was he like; what drove him; how was he treated; what did he do?)**

3. **Describe his living situation. Where was he living?**

4. **What did the man lose when Satan got a foothold into his life? Is there anything in the story to give you any clues about how Satan got a foothold?**

5. **What is significant about where he lived?**

6. **What was his life like after Jesus came?**

> **Scripture gives no explanation for Jesus' action regarding the pigs and, as He's the Sovereign God, none is required (see Job 38). But the root cause for the pigs' drowning was really someone else's poor choice. Human tragedy almost always results from sin. For example, global environmental damage can usually be traced back to man's actions rather than an "Act of God." War and governmental corruption impact worldwide starvation more than natural disasters.**

7. **Keep the perspective of this man's future in your focus. As the 'first missionary', his life was about to become much more focused and God-centered. How would the characteristics you noted in (2) above help him as he followed the new path Jesus forged for him?**

8. **Read Mark 5:15-20. What characteristics do you find in him now? Make a list of everything significant about his personality, how he was treated, what he was like and what drives him now as opposed to before Jesus' coming to his life.**

Divine Intervention

9. **Describe Jesus' encounter with the demon(s).**

10. **Record every word and action of the demons in this story.**

11. **Read Mark 5:6-8. "Son of the Most High God" is not a Messianic term but a divine one. Common to the day was the theory that using the precise name of an individual gave the user mastery over the person. What does this tell you about how Jesus confronted the demons and they Him?**

12. **Why do you think the demons wanted to stay in the area? (Mark 5:10)**

The demons didn't want to be forced to leave. They were comfortable inhabiting the man living in the places where death reigned. Perhaps this is something we should consider today. How comfortable do we make it for the enemy to take root in our homes, our children' lives and our own? Do you allow your children to listen to destructive music or wear clothing with skeletons and other dark forces? Do you dabble in the enemy's strongholds yourself? Do you think it matters? Beware of subtle things in life that open the door for the enemy.

Legion literally means 6,000. It conjures up a version of an occupying army – one bringing cruelty and destruction. That's a lot of misery packed into one life! The demon answered Jesus, "We are many."

Setting aside the demon possession element of the story for a moment, Lloyd Ogilvie in his study of Mark uses the phrase, "we are many" to point out that in our own lives we too have many forces in us driving us to make choices (not necessarily demons). He says that like a legion of soldiers, "…there are numberless appetites, desires, frustrations, fears, anger, hatreds, loyalties, dreams and aspirations in me that I cannot understand…We want to be loving, but so often we are hateful and envious…We want to serve Christ but are ambitious for security and position, for things we can taste and touch."[28]

13. **Think about this in terms of your own life today. How did Jesus help this man? How can He help you? Read Isa. 61:1-9. How does this passage address the legions we all deal with every day?**

14. **Read Mark 5:14-17. Scripture recorded the demon's name as "Legion". There is no doubt that the man was demon-possessed because Jesus declares he had an unclean spirit. Answer these questions from the text:**

   (a) **What did Jesus say to the demons? (:8)**

   (b) **What did the demons ask Jesus? (:10-11)**

   (c) **What did Jesus do in response? (:13)**

   (d) **What happened to the pigs? (:13)**

15. **What does the passage tell us about human need and how God sees people?**

---

[28] Ogilvie, IBID., 96-97.

Jesus and the Townspeople

Jesus has been criticized for destroying the property of the herdsmen by allowing the demons to inhabit and destroy the pigs. There are several possible explanations, but one thing we see clearly is that a man was freed and made whole. William Lane in his commentary on Mark says, "The fate of the swine demonstrates the ultimate intentions of demons with respect to the man they possessed. It is their purpose to destroy the creation of God. They were halted in their destruction of a man, but they fulfilled their purpose with the swine."[29] Think about this quote. What else could Jesus have done?

Isn't it ironic that the people were more frightened of Jesus than the demon-possessed man?

16. **Does this reveal where peoples' treasures lie – not in God or other people, but in their possessions? What about today?**

17. **Why do you think the people asked Jesus to leave?**

18. **Read Mark 5:19-20. The man wanted to go with Jesus. How did Jesus answer the man? Why do you think Jesus refused the man's request?**

Are you as exhausted as I am by today's study? We have walked in deep rivers today as we've looked inside a man's broken life, encountered a legion of demons, listened in as confused and broken people deny Jesus and forcefully tell Him to leave. We have encountered some deep philosophical questions that might leave us confused and wondering what it's all about.

We've even looked into our own 'legion' of problems to try to get some perspective. But I also trust you've gathered the cloak of hope around you as you have seen Who has the power over evil; Who has the power to save; Who has the power to change us from the inside out. He is the one Who will 'never leave us or forsake us.' Take heart from today's lesson.

In the next session we journey with Jesus and His disciples as they encounter more life and death issues.

---

[29] Lane, IBID. 180.

Day 5
Faith Concealed, Revealed and Rewarded (Mark 5:21-43)

Background Information

The disciples were once again on the trail with Jesus. Having left Decapolis they returned to Galilee by the same route, traveling over the Sea of Galilee. Jesus was once again pressed in by a great multitude when He was approached by one of the synagogue officials asking for help for his sick daughter.

On the way, Jesus was interrupted by one of the crowd, a woman who should not have been there because, according to Jewish law she was unclean and untouchable. But it was a new day and she had a divine appointment. The kingdom of heaven was at hand and the woman was pressing in to reach for it. God always honors our pressing in on Him to reach healing and change for the new season in our lives. It is what kingdom living is all about.

In this study we will see faith concealed, faith revealed and faith rewarded. But for Jairus, Jesus' interruption cost his daughter dearly and perhaps his own faith faltered. However, Jesus is ever and always intentional and He never wastes an opportunity to teach and touch. As Jesus would tutor Jairus and His disciples, kingdom living means that the grief of one season must be healed in order to walk into the new season. There is much to see and experience in today's lesson as we look at Jesus' power to heal and His authority over death.

Disciples' Perspective

Jesus ramped up things with the disciples as He allowed the encounters and interruptions of life to impact their day. Keep the disciples in mind as you are reading this section. What do they see, hear and experience? Do you think they learn well the principle that, "Life's interruptions are God's opportunities"?

Historical Quote

"God walks everywhere incognito. The world is crowded with God. We need to awaken to him."

-C.S. Lewis

Getting to the Heart of the Matter

Today's Reading: Read Mark 5:21-43
Parallel Passages: Matt. 9:18-26; Luke 8:40-56

"...the whole truth"

1. **What do we know from the passage about the woman with the issue of blood? Use the parallel passages at Matt. 9:18-22. Also review Lev. 15:19-**

27 to help you understand her desperation in even attempting to walk amongst the crowd.

2. What did the disciples learn about Jesus in this encounter with the woman?

3. Why do you think Jesus wanted the woman to admit or speak publicly about her experience?

4. Everything Jesus did was intentional. Had He allowed her to touch Him, get healed and disappear, she and others would have missed the blessing. What did those present (Jairus, the woman, the crowd) learn from this encounter?

5. In Mark 5:33 the passage says she told Jesus, "the whole truth." What was the whole truth from her perspective? What happens when we tell Jesus "the whole truth" about our situation? Are you holding something back from Him in your own life?

6. Her touch was expectant and persistent – what does this section teach about how to encounter Jesus in our own lives?

7. How did Jesus handle the interruption of His plans to travel with Jairus? How do you handle interruptions in your daily schedule?

8. Jesus sensed the difference between a touch by faith and the pressing of the crowd. What is significant about this for our lives today? (See Psalm 50:15)

9. **Once again the crowd was pressing on Jesus, not in faith, but for what they could get. What difference do you see between the woman and the crowd in general?**

10. **Not every touch of Jesus resulted in healing. What do you think made the difference here? And what practical application can it have for your life today?**

Jairus' Journey
Read Mark 5:35-43

11. **From today's reading, write out what we know of Jairus. Review Matt. 9:18-26 for additional help.**

12. **Jesus did not seem to be caught off-guard when the mourners told Jairus his daughter was dead. What did Jesus tell Jairus?**

Jairus just witnessed the connection between faith and divine healing – yet now he was asked to believe in the faith that his daughter would live despite the facts before him. Do you think you could believe what you were being told rather than what you could see with your own eyes? It is difficult, isn't it?

13. **Why do you think Jesus allowed only Jairus, his wife, Peter, James and John to attend Him as He met with the little girl?**

It has been quite a week, hasn't it? We've walked alongside Jesus as He told stories, calmed seas, healed a Gentile of unclean spirits, received a woman's faith as she was healed by touching Him and raised a little girl from the dead. No one who encountered Him that week would ever be the same.

But I wonder about now if some of you aren't questioning these dynamic stories as you try to bring them into alignment with your own life. "Why doesn't He heal me? I'm trying to touch the hem of His garment too. Why didn't God keep my child alive? Why are there so many troubles and trials in the world? I'm just not feeling the dynamics here!"

If that describes you, don't give up yet! You're not alone! In next week's lesson we will read some stories where it appeared as though God wasn't in control at all. We're going to take a look at what we can learn from failure.

Family Matters
This week I have two movie recommendations for you to rent:

- *Amazing Grace* -- the story of John Newton, slave-trader turned believer and his impact on William Wilberforce (played brilliantly by Ian Gruffold). It is a story that powerfully depicts what we've been studying this week – how encountering Christ can change a life.

- *The Ultimate Gift* – a prodigal son story about a young man from a wealthy family who expects to receive a great deal of money when his wealthy grandfather passes on. Instead of money he receives a series of tasks to complete, which change his life.

Looking Forward
Failures and Faith – How Jesus can even turn our failures into victory with a little dab of faith.

Chapter 4
Failures and Faith (Mark 6)

Day 1
What Happened to Faith? (Mark 6:1-6)

Personal Story

It feels like a gaping hole in our soul where the enemy has taken a giant dagger and thrust it in, twisting it in a gut-wrenching, slicing open of all that is raw and wounded inside of us. I stood on its precipice this very morning as once again I failed my husband and in some ways he failed me. We stood on the battleground, lines drawn in the sand, face to face with the pain of it until the rough edges wore down enough and we were finally able to reach across enemy lines, grab hands and talk it through.

But it is not always that simple. As we will see today, failure comes in all sizes and shapes. It hits us when we're down, attacks the most vulnerable places in our hearts, exposes our weaknesses, hinders relationships and sometimes locks out the only One who can heal us.

This week we look at failure in its different faces and forms. John the Baptist failed, "Are you really the One? Or should we keep looking?" Herod failed. His spirit was weak and his flesh weaker. The disciples failed. After over and over seeing, hearing and experiencing, they still could not believe.

Some say even Jesus failed when He went to His own hometown and was told to leave being unable to do any miracles other than a few healings because the people there lacked faith to see. But it wasn't Jesus who failed. The people of Nazareth failed because they saw Jesus the carpenter and missed seeing Jesus the Messiah. Their failure is so very much like ours.

You're in good company this week since all of us are in the fellowship of the failed. But don't give up – there are wondrous, marvelous things to be seen here – things to help us stand tall, take our failures by the throat and let the Spirit turn our mourning into joy, our lemons into lemonade.

Background Information

Jesus was at the peak of His ministry in this and the following few chapters. He was busy about His Father's business in fulfilling His mission to help people repent and believe (Mark 1:14-15). In the past few months much has happened – John was cruelly murdered, rumors about Jesus' identity were in abundance and the disciples were testing their wings.

Mark's gospel emphasizes the fact that Jesus performed His miracles in response to faith. Today is a story of faith failed and some needy people who missed the opportunity to be changed.

Disciples' Perspective

It was said of Napoleon that he had a great facility for victory but no strategy for failure. In this chapter we will see some examples of failure as we delve into Jesus' failure in Nazareth, His disciples' failure to trust and Herod's moral failures.

Mark shows us the truly difficult path in becoming a disciple – it was and is a slow and painful process. Even after they observed miracle after miracle and heard story after story, they still could not believe. God used failure to teach the disciples valuable lessons. In this study, keep your eye on the disciples.

Historical Quote

"Failure is not sin. Faithlessness is."

– Henrietta Mears

Getting to the Heart of the Matter

Today's Reading: Mark 6:1-6 Jesus returns to His hometown
Parallel passages: Matt. 13:53-58; Luke 4:14-21[30]

Review the parallel passage in Luke 4:14-21 and note what Scriptures Jesus preached on in the synagogue. By now Isaiah 61:1-4 should be a familiar passage to you. In preaching on this section Jesus is telling the people that He is the Messiah and this passage catalogues what His purpose in coming was to fulfill.

1. **In Luke 4:21 Jesus tells the people, "Today this Scripture has been fulfilled in your hearing." Do you think this statement had anything to do with His reception by the townspeople? Why or why not?**

---

[30] Some scholars say this Mark passage was the same as Luke 4:16-21; some say Jesus visited there twice and Luke's story was a different event.

2. Scripture reports in Mark 6:5-6 that it was not Jesus' power that is limited, but rather the unbelief of the people. Explore and write your thoughts on this idea of the tension between faith and unbelief using what you have learned in previous studies.

For some of you it just sits wrong to think that Jesus failed in anything. Actually you are correct. It wasn't His failure, but the people's lack of belief in Him. We must get our heads around the concept of faith. So much of kingdom living hinges on it.

3. Compare the people's reaction here to those in Mark 5:17. What is the difference between the two groups?

4. William Lane in his commentary on the gospel of Mark said of this section, "The performance of miracles in the absence of faith could have resulted only in the aggravation of human guilt and the hardening of men's hearts."[31] What do you think this means? Do you agree or disagree? Why? Can you think of any Scriptural principles to support your position?

> The word *astonished* in the Greek in verse 2 is *ekplesso*, the equivalent of the English word *flabbergasted*. Wuest says the word means, "to expel by a blow; to strike one out of self possession." In other words, "They were so astonished by his teaching to the point of losing control themselves." (Wuest 1973)

5. What lessons could the disciples learn by observing what happened in Nazareth?

6. What lessons could the Roman Christians learn from Mark's telling of this story?

7. What was the failure of the people and what can you learn from your conclusion?

8. How can we use what we have learned today to help those we serve?

---

[31] Lane, IBID., 204.

9. **Review this week's lesson and jot down one or two concepts or principles that you think would help you live out kingdom living principles.**

I don't know about you, but I feel terribly sorry for those souls in Nazareth who were so astonished at Jesus that they booted Him out of His own home town! It makes me want to shine up my own shield of faith so I'm ready for His next visitation. I don't want my faith to be a stumbling block to His movement in my life.

But in truth, once again, I find that I am no different than the people of Nazareth. I am with them in the fellowship of the failed. The real point is, they saw Jesus as "the carpenter" and missed the truth that He was the Messiah. Every single day of my life God is actively showing up, just as He went to Nazareth. Each and every day I fail to recognize Him working in and around me just as they did.

One scholar opined it was the town's own *lack of self esteem* that caused them to reject Him. The question, "Can anything good come out of Nazareth?" (John 1:46) was a scathing commentary on the whole town which was beaten down, scorned at, laughed at, smallest of the small, the least of the least – just like Jesus' own birthplace (See Mic. 5:2). When God comes to town we sometimes miss His coming because of our own darkness and lack of self-esteem.

And yet, we must not forget the kingdom principles we are learning. One is that He came to set the captives free, and it is in our captivity that we miss His coming. A second principle is that out of the smallest and least comes the biggest harvest, the best blessings, the greatest gain, the world-changers, the Savior.

It is a paradox and a principle that the people of Nazareth didn't understand. We MUST adjust our thinking to a Biblical perspective so we don't miss the obvious. As the children's song says, "If you want to be great in God's kingdom, learn to be the servant of all." It's what Jesus does. It is Who He is.

Day 2
I am Sending You (Mark 6:7-14)

Personal Illustration

The first time I went to court after passing the Bar I was sick for three days before appearing. I was standing in for another attorney on one of his cases. He carefully and patiently walked me through every possible scenario, every looming possible nightmare and I was still sick and scared. I had built up this case in my mind like it was the biggest case to ever hit Rancho Cucamonga. I researched and thought it through over and over. When the case was finally over, I think I made about $1.00 an hour! It was actually a simple, straightforward case where the other side wasn't even planning on showing up. As it turned out, I didn't even have to prove the case. I stood up, croaked out my name and the Judge, seeing my terror, took over, asked me a couple of questions, made a ruling and I was free. And I won the case! It doesn't get much better than that (and it didn't!).

In today's lesson, the disciples were out on their own with nary a security blanket between them. *They* would now be experiencing the failures of others' faith and the rejection of other Nazareths on their own journeys, but they would also be experiencing great joy as their own words and actions freed people and introduced them to the only One who could truly change them. Today we experience kingdom living on tour with the twelve!

Background Information

Down through the ages there have been hundreds and thousands who have followed Jesus' mandate to His disciples as they experienced their first mission trip. Some followed the letter of the law as seen in this section, but most followed the spirit of the law, going as the Spirit commanded.

Gladys Aylward (1902-1970) is one amazing example. A single woman, she was turned down by several missionary boards after applying to go to China. She knew she was called to go after reading a magazine article about China. After several rejections she returned home, spilled the contents of her purse and out of it two pennies fell on her Bible. She said, "O God, here's my Bible! Here's my money! Here's me! Use me, God." She scrimped and saved working as a maid in wealthy households until she had enough money to get a train into Asia. She took almost nothing with her. When the money ran out, the train dropped her off and she walked the rest of the way in to China. She had an amazing ministry and was a living example of what the disciples experienced.

Disciples Perspective

Can you imagine the disciples' thoughts on their first solo appearance? Who knew what could come up – think about the possible headlines: *Leper colony revolts, threatens to disband and fill streets; Demons run amuck in town square; Caesar's daughter sick – disciples called on to heal!* The possibilities are endless and the impossibilities of preparing for every situation, mind-boggling. Their worst nightmare lurking right around the corner. Sound familiar? We often don't wait for the future to get to us, but imagine the worst, and from my perspective, it doesn't always look good! Thankfully, I have some friends who don't see things quite the way I do. I need a dose of their friendship often to help me stay the course. The disciples already had the answer in their arsenal if they could just remember it: "With God all things are possible."

Historical Quote

"...God reveals His will and invites you to join Him where He is already working."
-Henry Blackaby

Getting to the Heart of the Matter

Today's Reading: Mark 6:7-14
Parallel Passages: Matt. 9:35-10:42; Luke 9:1-5

1. Jesus' goal from the beginning had been to equip the disciples in kingdom work. His first call to them was to be with Him and learn from Him. (Mark 3:13-6:6); the second call was to put into effect what they learned through listening and observing. What preparations have the disciples received from your study of this book so far?

2. How was Jesus growing their faith?

3. By allowing the disciples to take only what was necessary, Jesus was growing their faith by layers. Not only would they perform miracles, God would provide for them. Review Mark 6:7-13. List the tools the disciples were allowed to take, and note specifically what they were *not* allowed to take.

    Items the disciples could take   *Items they could not take*

4. From the passage, what one thing did Jesus specifically give to them to enable them to complete their task? (Mark 6:9)

5. Is there anything significant about the specific items they were not to take with them? What lessons were they were to learn from doing without?

6. From what you have learned so far, jot down a few ideas of what the disciples observed about:

   (a) Jesus

   (b) The people they ministered to

   (c) the power of God

7. Review the mission Jesus defined for the disciples in Mark 6:6-7. Is there anything contained in His assignment that He had not already demonstrated for them? What does this tell you about your mission today?

8. What does it mean to "shake the dust off of your sandals" in Mark 6:11? Why did Jesus instruct the disciples to do this in places where they were not welcomed?

9. Jewish law recognizes the commission (or assignment) of an individual as being the same as the one who commissioned him. What are the implications of this statement in this section of Scripture? How about today?

10. Review Mark 6:12-13. Identify what the disciples did. How did they know to do these things?

We need to address an important point about evangelism. It is clear from Scripture that the disciples had permission to leave if they were not wanted by any individual or village. It wasn't the disciples' failures any more than Jesus' reception at Nazareth was His. We need to understand this in terms of evangelism today. Too often we feel guilty that we do not share Christ with everyone we meet.

For instance, I feel particular guilt if I ignore the captive audience of a seatmate on an airplane. We need to understand that it is the Holy Spirit who draws people and grows the kingdom. Our job is to be the voice, hands, feet and ears when called by Him to do so. This means that we are to be watching, observing and listening to see where God is working in and around us. If someone is seeking, step in. If you are asked a spiritual question or even a question that could lead to a hint of a spiritual direction, consider it an open door. If you start a conversation trying to lead into a spiritual discussion and it is ignored, feel free to step out, shake off the dust and move on. Jesus sent out His disciples giving them permission to move on if there was no interest in kingdom living. It is the same today.

However, be sure you don't allow yourself to use this as a cop-out if a genuine opportunity is presented to you. The disciples would have missed a lot of blessing and growth opportunity had they turned a deaf ear to the calling. Evangelism is part of every believer's calling.

Day 3
The Parenthesis Concerning Herod (Mark 6:14-29)

Background Information

In the middle of cataloguing Jesus' various travels, Mark presents an excursus (a break in the story) to present a fuller account of what happened to John the Baptist. In doing so Mark gives us a clear picture of Herod Antipas, his household and his character. Actually, though the passage calls Herod "King", he was not a king, but a tetrarch (a leader of one-fourth of an empire).

Mark may have called him "king" either as an irony (because Herod badly wanted to be a king) or as the local custom. Herod was also a Jew by birth though nothing in the passages about him indicates that he followed his heritage. He was married to the daughter of King Aretas (from a kingdom east of where Herod's tetrarchy lay, presumably married to expand his border and secure an ally, a not uncommon reason for marrying then).

While a guest of his half-brother, Herod Phillip, Herod Antipas met and fell in love with Phillip's wife, Herodias. He and Herodias plotted to leave their spouses and marry each other. A Jew was forbidden to marry his brother's wife if the brother was still alive. (Lev. 18:16, 20:21) This may have been what brought Herod Antipas and Herodias to John's attention. Antipas sent his first wife, King Aretas' daughter away and brought Herodias to the palace. When John renounced their relationship, Herodias was infuriated and sought ways to keep him away from her new husband, who was in a strange way fascinated by John and his teaching. She eventually brought about John's death.

Both Herod Antipas and his new wife were flawed characters, not unlike the rest of us in some ways. But they were unredeemed flawed characters. For all of the trappings of success and prestige around him, Herod was a spiritual failure.

Scripture tells us that Herod was interested in spiritual things (Mark 6:20), but in beheading John the Baptist, he silenced the voice of truth. The guilt of this and his continued lifestyle led him into bondage that none but the One and only could deliver him from. One scholar said that in a "loose sense, Herod believed", but recall our study in Mark 1:24 where we learned that the "demons also believe" (James 2:19). As we have also been learning, in kingdom living, mere belief isn't enough unless the belief changes how we live.

People's curiosity about God, much like Herod's, might be intriguing but unless it changes them, and they let Him into their lives to clean out the soul and make all things new, it would not help them. Herod's life remained unchanged by God's coming. It was Herod's choice of whether to listen to John the Baptist or merely have "his ears tickled."

Disciples' Perspective

When studying Scripture, we must understand that every word and every story can be looked at in a myriad of different ways. I like to say that Scripture is like an onion (and I said it way before *Shrek* was ever in the theatres) and there are layers and layers of ways which we can view the Scriptures. In this story, for example, Herod's life could be looked at and studied from the perspective of "Leadership Fails," "The Consequences of Poor Choices," or from the perspective of a preacher (John) and his hearer (Herod). As disciples we need to know the Scripture and observe and listen to people's lives to discern how particular passages will touch them. The Holy Spirit will guide us as we seek His direction.

Historical Quote

"Failure is not falling down, but staying down."
-Mary Pickford

Getting to the Heart of the Matter

Today's Reading: Mark 6:14-29
Parallel Passages: Matt. 14:1-12; Luke 9:7-9

1. **Review Mark 6:14-29. Make a list of qualities you see in Herod, both good and bad. This exercise is worth our time because the character qualities you see in him are present today. We are all a mix of good/bad qualities.**

Good qualities   *Bad qualities*

2. From what you've read, what soil do you think is representative of Herod's heart? You may need to review Mark 4 and the four soils mentioned.

3. List the five statements made by Herod himself in this section. What does each statement tell you about his character?

4. What three things were people saying about Jesus in Mark 6:14-15?

5. In Mark 6:16 Herod believed Jesus was John risen from the dead. Why did he believe this rather than the other rumors?

6. In Jewish thinking, resurrection is a prelude to judgment. That terror is caught by Herod's repeated statement, "It is John, whom I beheaded, who is now risen." (Mark 6:16) What does this express about Herod's state of mind?

7. Define people pressure or peer pressure. There are always attempts by people to mold us, shape us and compel us to do things differently or their way. In some forms (such as mentoring) pressure can be good. What kind of pressure was brought to bear on Herod by the different people in the passage? How did he handle it? Give specific illustrations.

   (a) Herodias

   (b) Salome

   (c) Herod's guests

   (d) Herod Himself

   (e) God through John the Baptist

When I was a young believer and worked in my first law office, I worked for an attorney who was quite fascinated with my belief in God. He was also terrified by it. We talked for hours about life, death, heaven, hell and particularly Jesus. He wanted to hear and discuss it, but didn't want to commit to it. I prayed for him fervently and when, as he put it, "everything is going wrong in my life," he asked me to stop praying. I continued to pray for him but as the years went on, we lost contact and though I didn't stop praying until I heard he had died, I never knew the final outcome of our many conversations. There are lots of people like that. What recommendations would you have for me as a young believer in talking with this man?

The next questions probe motive and how sin propels us. Few understand the depth and pull that pride and other sins have on us. Scripture gives many examples of how sin drives and often overcomes us. By using Scriptural biography we can learn about ourselves and other people through the lives we see in Scripture.

Salome's Request
Read Mark 6:21-29.

8. **Even if Herod didn't want to do what Salome asked of him he felt unable to deny her. Why?**

9. **Did Herod have a choice after Salome gave her request? How could he have gotten around what was being asked?**

10. **What kept him from looking at other options?**

11. **Read Psalm 32:5-7 written by David after his sin with Bathsheba. (2 Samuel 11) Compare David's situation to Herod's sin of murder. How did the way David handled the situation differ from Herod?**

Herod Antipas actually came to a bad end. Revenge and bitterness are strong tools in the arsenal of a king or anyone else with power. Herod's ex-wife's father, King Aretas, mounted an attack against Herod and wiped out his entire army. Later, as Josephus in *Antiquities* tells us, Herod's ambition for the title king led to his dismissal and exile by the Emperor Caligula in AD 39.

What happens to us when the voice of truth whispers about a hidden sin or addiction? This is an important question because so many people today, even in churches, live double lives. There are pornographers, abusers, murderers, liars, cheats, gossips, adulterers and if I went on, we could all find ourselves somewhere on the list if we haven't already. It is not so much that we are caught by these sins as it is by what we do about it. Do we throw ourselves on God's mercy and grace or does pride rise up and throw a cloak over us enabling us continue to live in our pet sin, hide it, harbor it and engage in it until it and the associated guilt of leading a double life destroys us or others whom it touches?

Such was the fate of Hester Prynne's lover in Nathaniel Hawthorne's *The Scarlett Letter*. *[If you plan to watch the movie or haven't read the book, skip the next line]*. He was after all, a man of the cloth, a clergyman. If his sin with an unmarried woman became known his life, his career and all that he worked for, would be over. It was over anyway. His unconfessed sin of adultery together with his signature sin of pride destroyed him, much as it did Herod. It is a tragic story of failure on so many levels.

Day 4
Being Sent (Mark 6:30-44)

Background Information

From a 1937 commentary in German, William Lane quotes "In the midst of the wilderness, among the sheep without a shepherd, there stands one who breaks bread; the Messianic feast transcends realism and its confusions. God's kingdom opens, they eat, and are filled without knowing how."[32] This is a good summary of our reading today and is recognizable as to how God works in our own lives. Most of us focus on the "without knowing how" part and miss the miracle.

In this section the disciples reported to Jesus all that they had done and taught in their first missionary journey (Mark 6:7-13). Jesus, recognizing their need for rest, sent them to the wilderness place also called the *desert* in Greek. There they were pursued by desperate crowds wanting more as they recognized them. Welcome to the world of the called! As so often is the case, the disciples went from the heights of excitement regarding everything accomplished on their journey, to the depths of despair as they once again fell into failure and doubt. I'm so glad Scripture records things just the way they are. It gives me hope for my own flawed journey and future in the kingdom.

> The *wilderness* journey – (whether Jews wandering in the Arabian desert for 40 years, or captivity in Assyria and Babylon, or Mark's Christian readers in the wilderness of persecution in Rome) – is the believer's experience and a consistent theme throughout Mark and the Scripture. *Sabbath rest* is the believer's peace and renewal experienced in the midst of the wilderness journey.

---

[32] Lane, IBID., 231.

Disciples' Perspective

Today's reading is all about the disciples. For the first time they found themselves the pursued ones by the crowd. Jesus actively involved the disciples in every step of the day's activities. However, they were at a loss on how to proceed when their Teacher gently suggested that since the crowd was following them, it was for them to take care of the needs. His words baffled them, His actions of divine power stalled them and though they had just returned from a miraculous journey using the very power He gave to them, they did not understand Him.

I've been known a time or two to respond in exactly the same way, and I suspect you're in this with me: "What? Me? Are you kidding, I can't do that!" You will also probably see yourself mirrored in their panic. Thankfully we both have the same Teacher and, like the disciples, He will use the panicked, impossible demands in our own lives to gently lead us, teach us and draw us deeper into kingdom living.

Historical Quote

Earth is crammed with Heaven
And every common bush afire with God,
but only he who sees takes off his shoes.

The rest sit round it and pluck blackberries.
                    -Elizabeth Barrett Browning

Getting to the Heart of the Matter

Today's Reading Mark 6:30-44
Parallel Passages: Matt. 14:13-21, Luke 9:10-17, John 6:1-15

1. **From Mark 6:30-32, where did Jesus send the disciples? Was there any significance to the place they were to go?**

Rest is an important discipline in a believer's life, even though at times it seems as though it is not always possible. God rested after creating the world which gives us our mandate. In previous passages we've seen how Jesus often withdrew to a "lonely place" (Mark 1:35) to rest and pray. Now He is teaching the disciples this discipline.

2. **Do you think rest is still an important discipline today? Why or why not?**

> The meaning of *rest* in the Greek is "to cause or permit one to cease from labor in order to recover and collect his strength."

3. Evaluate this statement: "Life's interruptions are God's opportunities." We've seen it before in this study. Notice what happened to Jesus and the disciples in their attempt to find rest. How did Jesus deal with this interruption in Mark 6:34?

4. What did He do for the masses that came to Him?

5. How did the disciples handle the situation? (Mark 6:35-36) (Recall they were probably tired from their own journey.)

Keeping the Sabbath is not only one of the Ten Commandments but is given to us as a gift.

6. What does Sabbath rest look like to you? What things in your life would you need to adjust to incorporate rest into your life?

How much Sabbath rest are you experiencing in your life which enables you to recover and collect your strength? How often are you able to do this in a six-month time-frame? Is it enough? Rest is not always possible, which is why we need to clear time on our schedules to practice the discipline. Make a plan or a goal to carve out more time for this activity.

> The sum of hundred denarius is about a year's wage for a worker. Jesus seemed always to be asking the impossible of His disciples.

7. In Mark 6:33, who was the crowd pursuing this time? From the context of this verse, do you think the crowd had time to prepare for this meeting or was it spontaneous? Support your answer with the Scripture.

8. How did Jesus respond when He saw the crowd? (Mark 6:34)

Feeding the People

After returning from their great victory, the disciples were given a big challenge. In Mark 6:35-38 Jesus commanded them to feed 5000 people with basically nothing.

9. **What was the disciples' response to the feeding command? What happened to the disciples here?**

10. **Have you ever been asked to do a seemingly impossible task? Write out your thoughts on this.**

Notice from this story how Jesus never wasted an opportunity to teach a principle while meeting the needs of others. He was teaching the disciples important lessons too.

11. **What things did Jesus teach the disciples in this passage?**

12. **What was their response?**

13. **We've seen several times in our study that the crowds followed Jesus for what they could get from Him but many did not really commit their lives to His call. Still, Jesus kept teaching, touching, healing, blessing and seeking out the lost. What lessons can we learn today from how He ministered to those who were nominally interested in Him?**

Don't you love how Jesus teaches? He sent the disciples out to survey the impossibility of the situation in feeding five thousand people with five loaves of bread and two fish and He let them figure it out. When they failed, He didn't chide them. He looked to heaven and prayed. And they watched and learned.

Years ago I had an experience as a volunteer staff person in a Christian youth organization. I attended a staff retreat and because I was new, I was not well known. About 35 people attended the retreat. Our weekend retreat was in the local mountains in February. Snow time in Southern California! The itinerary included "snow play," so in mid to late afternoon we loaded on to a bus and went to an open field to engage in snow sports. Two other new girls and I decided to take a walk into the trees to explore a bit.

When we returned a short time later, everyone was gone. We looked at one another in astonishment and horror. We didn't even know the name of the retreat center. How were we going to find our way back? *"How many loaves and fishes do you have?"* We had nothing – no phone numbers, no phones (before the days of cell phones), and no sense of direction. As the oldest of the group (I was about 20), the girls looked to me for a solution. It was getting dark and colder by the minute. I wanted to sit down and cry. Instead I said, "Well, let's start walking." And we walked and walked, and finally, timidly, one of us suggested, "Maybe we better pray." So, having nothing to lose and everything to gain, we tried that.

Within about 10 minutes we saw headlights approaching and flagged down the car. Thankfully and amazingly, it was a police car. He found out where we belonged and transported us to our unknown location. There's more to the story, which I will save for another time, but I tell you this as a parallel to today's story. "How will you feed them?" "How will you get home?" The answer to both questions is the same.

Day 5
Faith Stretching (Mark 6:45-56)

Background Information

Jesus continued to stretch the disciples' faith in today's lesson when He left them alone in the middle of the lake while He went to the mountains to pray. After feeding 5000 people with just a few loaves and fish, there was a movement by the people to make Jesus their king and usher in the kingdom right then. (John 6:14-15) It was not the Father's timing, which was perhaps why Jesus dispersed the crowd and sent the disciples on so He could pray and discern God's will.

Mark was very good about setting the scene and in this event He tells us that during the fourth watch of the night (between 3:00-6:00 a.m.) the disciples ran into problems on the sea. Jesus, seeing them from the shore, went to them walking on water.

I would love to be a fly on your wall as you explore this section of Scripture to see what you are learning about discipleship. There are several lessons we can learn about how Jesus stilled their fears, calmed the storm and led them directly into an encouraging, heart lifting early morning healing service. But not before their "little faith" had a chance to grow by a great leap. It is how our little faith grows too.

Disciples Perspective

When the disciples were without Jesus, they were distressed and lacking in faith. But as we saw in yesterday's study, even when He was with them they sometimes didn't see and understand. Once again Jesus wanted to strengthen their faith. In the darkness of early morning they were deceived by their eyes. It was only when He spoke that they recognized the beloved Voice. Scripture today tells us their hearts were hardened due to lack of understanding. Jesus didn't give up on them and He won't give up on us.

Historical Quote

"Faith itself is a risk. You must trust God and act in faith to take that step you cannot see. If you're going to walk on water, you need to be willing to take chances that you might hit rock bottom."[33]

-William Backus.

Getting to the Heart of the Matter

Today's Reading: Mark 6:45-56
Parallel Passages: Matt. 14:22-36; John 6:16-24

1. **What time did the events here occur? (Mark 6:46-47)**

Recall in an earlier chapter we discussed the image of the church as the boat in a stormy sea to give comfort to the suffering Roman believers. Here is the picture again to reinforce it in our minds. While the disciples were straining at the oars in the boat, where was Jesus? Do you think He was praying for the disciples? If so, even in their own stress and strain, and even though they were unaware, there was a "heavenly watcher" in whose Hand they rested.

2. **What principles can you draw from this picture of Jesus as the *heavenly watcher*?**

It is always to the Voice of Truth that we must listen. Studying Scripture such as this Bible study and others will help you discern the voice in your own life. In this story, the disciples' failure was not that they had no faith, but that it was small compared to what they had already been given by Jesus. This describes many of us. It is only as we "stay the course" that our faith can grow.

3. **Herod wasn't the only one who was a superstitious Jew. When the disciples saw Jesus walking on water, what did they think?**

4. **When did they realize Who it was? (Mark 6:50)**

---

[33] William Backus and Marie Chapian, *Telling Yourself the Truth,* (Minneapolis: Bethany House, 1985)

5. Notice the pattern: whenever the Master was absent from the disciples (or appeared to be), they found themselves in distress. Is there a lesson in this principle?

6. How did Jesus use this event, coupled with the other events connected in Mark 5-6 to teach the disciples? What do you think He wanted them to know foremost?

7. Read Mark 6:52. Compare it with Proverbs 4:23 and 1 Samuel 16:7. Note your observations.

8. What characteristics of Christ do you see in this passage? (Mark 6:45-56) (Also refer to Job 9:8)

How much like the disciples we are: tired and toiling, rowing against the wind, feeling forlorn and forgotten. Yet Scripture tells us that Jesus *saw* them from the shore and began walking toward them. Note that He came to them in the middle of the night when doubts are strongest. He came in the midst of the storm in the middle of the lake to teach them to recognize God moving in and around their lives. When Jesus says in the midst of your storm, "It is I", it is a call to faith. When He says, "Don't be afraid." It is a call to action.

9. What do you think the disciples' state of mind and body was during this time? (Recall that they had not received the rest they anticipated after returning from their missionary journey). [Mark 6:32-33].

10. Hendriksen says our faith, "…should be sufficiently wide awake to derive legitimate conclusions from firmly established premises…"[34] What do you think he means by this?

11. I hope your faith has grown as you have taken the lessons you've learned in your study of Mark's gospel so far. Take a moment here to jot down a few things you remember about what you've studied in this chapter.

---

[34] Hendriksen, IBID., 263.

While the disciples understood Jesus' instruction in the feeding of the 5000, they didn't understand the deeper walk – that through Jesus, God was showing up. When He came in another unexpected way they missed His coming again. Their misunderstanding reflected their unbelief. Perhaps you might be thinking, "How could they have NOT seen, understood, believed?" How many times have you and I said, "If I saw a real miracle, I would never doubt again!"? Hopefully that would be true, but Scripture seems to point to the fact that faith isn't immediately poured into us because of one thing, but it grows day by day, moment by moment, step by step as we put our hand into His and let Him lead the way.

Evangelist D.L. Moody said, "I prayed for faith and thought that someday faith would come down and strike me like lightning. But faith did not seem to come. One day I read the tenth chapter of Romans, 'Faith comes by hearing, and hearing by the Word of God.' I had up to this time closed my Bible and prayed for faith. I now opened my Bible and began to study, and faith has been growing ever since."

Today's failure of faith can be the raw materials for tomorrow's dependence on God and growth. Failure can lead to faith. It can also soften our critical spirit toward others. As you think of some of your recent failures, try to reframe them based on what you have learned about Jesus this week. Pray for God to expose the lies you have been living in the context of failure.

Family Matters

I have three movie recommendations this week:

- *The Inn of the Sixth Happiness* –a lovely story starring Ingrid Bergman about the life of Gladys Aylward and her impact in China. (I remember one cozy New Year's Eve when our plans went awry. We happened to have this movie available and all loved it. It was a most memorable family evening.)
- *Gifted Hands: The Ben Carson Story* -- a portrayal of the life of pediatric neurosurgeon Ben Carson who overcame enormous obstacles to study medicine and save lives at Johns Hopkins Hospital. (I am a sitting duck for over-comer movies and stories about people who face mountains and try to scale them. You won't regret checking this movie out.)
- *The Scarlett Letter* (*Meg Foster's version*) – about a young girl in puritan era Boston who becomes pregnant out-of-wedlock. Based on Nathaniel Hawthorne's novel of the same name. Her moral failure is her making, but her secret lover fares poorly. Because his sin is not exposed and dealt with, he lives with its secret which eats away at him. It is a moving, moralistic tale which has a lot to teach us about seeking forgiveness and allowing God to use our own failures for His best. Better than the movie,

read the book! While I don't recommend it for young children because of the mature theme, it has a strong moral message and is worth watching.

Also, listen to the lyrics of the song, The Voice of Truth by Casting Crowns. It is one of my favorite songs of all time. It helps me stand for and hear the Truth.

Looking forward
An opportunity to see what 'truth twisting' looks like so you will recognize it when you see it!

Chapter 5
Learning How to See (Mark 7-8)

Day 1
When Seeing Malfunctions: Truth Twisting (Mark 7:1-13)

Personal Illustration

As I have poured over this chapter it is one that touches me deeply and personally because I've been caught in the pharisaical tradition trap myself.

A number of years ago the church we were attending church switched from hymns to a more contemporary music style with drums and guitars. I didn't like it. I liked hymns because I knew all those songs and could worship loudly (and probably out of tune). I wrote about it in my journal; I griped about it to my husband and I even started coming to church 20 minutes later so I would miss the music. After all, how could I worship with all the noise?

One Sunday I needed to get to church early and didn't have an excuse for coming in late. I sat in my usual spot (more tradition!) and as I was sitting there with my arms crossed thinking in my heart how I disliked the whole thing, I heard an audible voice in my head. It said simply this: "It's not about you!" There was not a single doubt in my mind Who had spoken those words to me. It ended right there. I never again criticized any type of worship – no matter how different it was. I understood in an instant that worship is what comes out of the heart and it is *for God*, not for me, the worshiper.

Now when I hear or see others worshiping differently than I, I rejoice in it. I am thrilled when people worship God in a way that brings glory to Him. Years later when I was invited to join the staff, I was a proponent of all kinds of worship that caused people to seek Him in their own walk, not just traditional or contemporary, but in many ways.

One woman at our church worshiped through performing hula with a group not connected with our church. Their group blessed many people and turned their hearts heaven-ward. I asked her to bring it to our women's ministry. So many women were blessed as they found a new outlet to bring Him glory. Others were blessed and touched as they watched and listened. And God received a much-needed moment of rest as the sweet aroma of those women's worship rose heavenward.

Background Information

The crucifixion is in sight. From this point scholars believe it was about a year away. We have already seen in previous studies how Jesus differed with the Pharisees on points of what defines godliness (dining with outcasts, Mark 2:15-17; fasting, Mark 2:18-22 and observing the Sabbath, Mark 2:23-28). Here again the Pharisees confronted Jesus, this time concerning His disregard for the whole structure of oral tradition. As Jesus tried to show them, the Pharisees were replacing truth with tradition.

In areas where the law was silent, vocal tradition arose. In part of this section the dispute was over ceremonial hand-washing. There actually *was* a Biblical mandate for hand washing (Ex. 30:18-21), but it was directed at *priests*, not the general populace. It became a widespread practice that eventually was handed down orally for all to follow.

The Pharisees surpassed even the priests in their zeal. In the process they passed the regulations on to the laity and considered it the obligation of every Jew to so cleanse themselves. In their defense, the Pharisees intended their restrictions as an example to non-Jews to show that all Israel was devoted to God (Lev. 20:26). This was how they acknowledged and served God. But even good intentions can corrupt when the heart is not in it. This was precisely Jesus' point when He exposed their hypocrisy in the corban (Mark 7:9-13).

Corban is a term that means "sacred gift" or "anything set aside and dedicated to God." The way it was used, however, was as a religious excuse for sons who did not want responsibility for their parents. The Pharisees found a way around the fifth commandment to honor your father and mother. Honoring was more than taking care of a parent. If a son had property or possessions that were needed by the parent and the son didn't want to let it go, he had only to say, "It is corban" to preclude the parents from using it.

Once made, even in a fit of anger, the covenant could not be broken and the corban could never be used by the parents. The unjust part was that a son who declared corban was not precluded from using the item or property for himself. He could simply keep the parents from benefitting. This gave rise to all kinds of abuse by greedy children.

Jesus brought this up to show how man-made traditions can often circumvent the very Word of God and be so misused as to become a disgrace to a nation. It went against God's very desires and heart. We too have laws and traditions that similarly impact our culture and society today.

Disciples' Perspective

As the disciples continued to observe and absorb what Jesus was teaching, they were learning that Jesus wasn't teaching that tradition had no value. On the contrary, it is of immense value to help ground our faith, our family and our cultural experiences. Jesus took exception to *replacing* truth and faith with *man's traditions* or twisting it to suit their own purposes. The Pharisees elevated tradition making it synonymous with truth, and in some instances, such as the corban, offering a way *around the truth*.

They simply could not see that their man-made traditions were exploiting people, twisting the truth and was empty, shallow and of no value in the kingdom. The reality of this passage is that Jesus told us that all of these external rules were symbolic of a more important internal rule: *Is your heart prepared to come into God's presence?*

Historical Quote

"Christian activity never stems from the imperative of a divine command, but from the impulse of an indwelling Presence."
                                        -Ray Stedman

Getting to the Heart of the Matter

Today's Reading: Mark 7:1-13
Parallel passages: Matt. 15:1-10

In today's reading things were heating up for Jesus as Pharisees and scribes came from Jerusalem to confront Him. The minor hand washing infraction was just a point of contact for the Pharisees. Actually, Jesus was taking on the whole structure of oral tradition which regulated every aspect of personal and corporate life for the Jews.

This concerned religious leaders because His words were gaining authority with the people and in His words rested the fate of their own religious order. He was, in a sense, turning things inside out or outside in by His teachings.

Kingdom living highlights the importance of internal living and associates religion with understanding, not tradition or blind obedience. Jesus taught intentional kingdom living by bringing us face to face with our choices and showing how those choices impact our life. We can't get a pass by saying, "this is how it has always been done."

To understand the kind of obedience God wants from His disciples, consider this example: In my marriage, I don't want my husband to bring me flowers or do things for me because he has to do them. That doesn't speak love to me. I want him to do things because he thinks about me when I'm not with him; because he loves me deeply and wants to bring me joy, and because he wants to see my joy and my understanding of his love for me when he brings them.

If he had to bring me flowers because I expected them or he had no choice, that wouldn't be love from the depths. It is the same with worship. Do I have to worship God as a believer? Well – yes, but the worship God desires is not the have to kind, but the want to kind. There is no value in flowers or worship that don't come from a heart of love and a desire to bring joy to the one being loved.

1. **In Mark 7:1-6, write down what the Pharisees *saw*.**

2. **In Mark 7:1-6, write down everything the Pharisees *said*.**

3. **In Mark 7:6-8, what did Jesus say in response? What truths do you think Jesus was trying to show the Pharisees?**

4. **According to Jesus in Mark 7:6-13, what were the Pharisees teaching the people?**

Review Mark 7:6. *Hypocrite* comes from a Greek word which means mask. In early Greek dramas actors would wear masks to clarify the type of character they played. You may have seen the happy-sad mask which signifies the theater today.

5. **Define a hypocrite in your own words.**

6. **Now define where in life hypocrites are found. (HINT: If you said only church, think again.)**

7. **Why do you think Jesus was so forceful in His declaration against hypocrisy in this portion of Scripture?**

8. **How did Jesus use the Pharisees as a parable ("an earthly story with a heavenly meaning") in this passage?**

9. **What was missing from the Pharisees' lives as they tried to live for God outwardly? How did Jesus address this issue with them?**

Read Mark 7:9-13. *Corban* was designed to let sons save face when they didn't want responsibility for their parents. It was a way of getting out from under responsibility and looking good at the same time. Actually, it was an internal truth twisting.

If a son called corban, two things happened: (1) The son was no longer responsible to care for his parents: "I can't help my parents because everything I have is devoted to God." And, (2) The son looked good outwardly because it appeared as though he was totally devoted to God by "giving Him everything." The catch was he could actually use what was devoted to God for his own use – just not for his parents' use.

10. **What is wrong with this idea (corban)? Do you think people today use the concept of corban to get out from under responsibility? How? Give some examples.**

11. **Read Mark 7:1-13. Do you see any other truths that were being twisted? If so, record them here.**

12. **Jesus' first challenge to the Pharisees was to examine their hearts because obedience coming from any source but the heart was worthless. How did they handle this challenge from Jesus?**

13. **Explore your own hypocrisy – Are you tradition bound? Are you bothered:**

    (a) **When a song is sung in a style you don't like?**

    (b) **When a different kind of preaching than you're used to is presented?**

    (c) **When a newcomer sits in your accustomed place on Sunday morning?**

14. **What traditions and prejudices do you have that keep you from loving and helping certain people or groups?**

Often people today are on either side of the tradition debate. Some people are anti-tradition and despise all tradition. Others insist things be done exactly the same way they have always been done.

15. **In thinking through your own biases on this issue, finish this statement: "It just wouldn't be a worship service unless we …."**

All of us in some ways "truth-twist" even when we don't mean to. The Pharisees did it to protect the comfortable way of life they formed out of the mortar and stone of the Law. But it wasn't true and it wasn't real. Confrontation with Jesus turned them inward which was not a secure place for them so they got angry and frustrated, lashing out, wishing to kill Him.

When we get pinned to the wall in an area of our own discomfort, we do pretty much the same thing. Like a wounded, wild animal, we too strike out of our pain. That can sometimes be the catalyst for change, but not always, as was true in the case of the Pharisees. They lived outwardly impeccable lives, but it was a lie because they could not continue it inwardly. Without the help of the Holy Spirit none of us can.

You don't have to dress a certain way, talk a certain way or carry a particular Bible or any Bible to get into the kingdom. All you need is a rebellious heart (which we all have) that desires to be changed by God. Desire for change is what the Pharisees lacked. Where are you at in this process? Remember that the essential purpose of our being is to bring the heart of God into touch with the hearts of men (including ourselves).

Oh my friends, have you been able to see what I've missed in this chapter until now? That corban refers to a gift – anything that is set aside and dedicated to God. *You are the gift.* You and I are the ones He has called, set aside and dedicated to Himself. If corban refers to resources of God set aside for His purposes, that defines you and me. Our lives are corban – gifts to be used by God to bless others.

Day 2
The Me I Don't Want to See (Mark 7:14-23)

Background Information

I once heard or read a story about a holocaust survivor who was required to face the man who terrorized him and others in a concentration camp. I have never forgotten the story. As he was being led into the courtroom he came face to face with his torturer. He stood for a long minute looking at the man who killed his family and friends, tortured fellow Jews, sent them to gas chambers and caused the man himself to live a life of horror, misery and despair. To everyone's amazement, the man fell over in a faint. "It is understandable," said the experts, "coming face to face with his tormenter, his response is not surprising." What was surprising however, was when the man recovered and was questioned, it was not his tormenter who caused him such shock. "I looked into his eyes and I saw myself," said the man, "I saw all that I was capable of doing to others in that man's eyes."

It's in all of us – the potential to do great harm and to sin greatly. Never can we say, "I would never…" because we don't know what we are capable of in our hearts. Jer. 17:9 says, "The heart is more deceitful than all else, and is desperately sick; who can understand it?" (NASB)

This is Jesus' message in today's study. It is not how we look on the outside or what rules we follow, but He tries to focus us on what is coming out of our hearts.

The ultimate test of any tradition, any discipline is, "Does it deal with our heart issues? Does it expose areas we hoard and hide from God? Does it penetrate our lives to help us see God more clearly?"

Please understand. I'm not talking about holidays or traditions that define and communicate family, community and create unity. I'm talking about deeply held beliefs about what we must and must not do to be called Christians. It is those things that distract us from the truth and get us off-track from what is really important.

Jesus taught that when tradition becomes more important than the truth it represents or when it supersedes what God's Word says, we must tread carefully. We need eyes to see and ears to hear so that we can recognize our own truth-twisting.

In today's lesson, Jesus began to explain how to do this and He did it by taking on the heart. Jesus laid bare the lie that conformity from the outside is enough when in fact it breeds hypocrisy. He peels away the protective layers we wrap around our hearts to expose the anarchy and desperate wickedness that we are all capable of. He exposes our heart to clean us from the inside out, to make us whole and enable us to walk in the light of His kingdom.

Disciples' Perspective

The disciples were Jews raised in the same traditions of the people. They followed the law and the interpretations of the law as best they could. I'm sure if we could poll them, we would find some of them were uncomfortable with this new life. Jesus was declaring all foods clean, was not following the Mishnah (the collection of oral traditions in the Talmud), and was turning everything upside down. What were they to make of this new lifestyle? What would become of it?

Historical Quote

"There is enough tinder in the heart of the best of men in the world to light a fire that shall burn to the lowest hell, unless God should quench the sparks as they fall."
– C.H. Spurgeon

Getting to the Heart of the Matter

In this study, we will separately look at how the multitudes and the disciples responded to Jesus' teaching.

Today's Reading:Mark 7:14-23
Parallel passages: Matt. 15:10-20

The multitudes: Mark 7:14-16 and use Matt. 15:10-11 to supplement.
1. **Review Mark 7:1-23. Circle the word *heart* in each verse. What does each verse say about it?**

2. **What was the central lesson Jesus was trying to teach in this chapter?**

3. **Explore Mark 7:15. What did Jesus mean by the statement addressed to the multitudes?**

4. **Do you think He was saying the same thing to the Pharisees?**

5. **How about the disciples?**

6. Come up with a response to this statement from someone who does not attend church: "I'm not going to church. They are nothing but a bunch of hypocrites." (Preferably, don't use this response: *"Why don't you join us? One more won't hurt,"* though it's probably a true statement.)

The Disciples: Mark 7:17-23 and use Matt. 15:12-20 to supplement.

7. What was the central message to the disciples in Mark 7:17-23? How did it differ from the message Jesus gave to the multitudes? The Pharisees?

8. Review the catalog of things which come out of the heart in Mark 7:21-22. What types of corruption grows out of an impure heart?

9. List all twelve words, separating deeds from attitudes. Define any words you do not understand by using a dictionary.

10. Of the twelve words defined above, list one or two areas that you struggle with. How can what you are learning about kingdom living help you get freedom from these areas?

11. Why do you think Jesus gave this message to the disciples and not the other two groups? What practical reasons do you see?

12. How did the message Jesus gave the disciples help them in their path of following Him and learning from Him?

13. Give an example of how we replace God's truth with man's tradition today?

I don't like to think about the sin I harbor in my heart as expressed by the terrible twelve listed in Mark 7:21-22, but I'm inescapably a sinner – the lowest and least likely person to be called upon to represent a pure and Holy God. Yet it is people like me and you He reaches down to pull out of the mud, clothe in His own righteousness and put to work. These grimy hands, this filthy mouth, this desperately wicked heart, when surrendered to Him can bring Good News to a lost soul, forgive a wrong done or reach out and touch a life forever. Not by my own strength, but by the power of the One who lives in me.

Day 3
Seeing Those Who are Different (Mark 7:24-37)

Background Information

The background information today is so important in helping us understand this part of Jesus' mission. I don't want you to overlook it. After Jesus' confrontation with the Pharisees in Mark 6-7, He left the Jews and traveled with His disciples into Gentile country. Other than an earlier jaunt into Decapolis (which was populated by Gentiles and Jews alike), He had not ventured so far afield.

A cursory reading of Jesus' encounter with the Syrophoenician woman of today's lesson has led some to speculate on whether the shadow of racism was present in this story. Such a ridiculous claim is completely undone by Jesus' character and reveals how we often put our own cultural spin and societal mores on everything we encounter. Essentially Jesus told the woman what the current Jewish thinking was concerning Gentiles and asked her how she would respond to such a derogatory opinion. He may have been mirroring the disciples' thinking toward Gentiles and beginning to unravel their hold on the outdated traditions and biases they were brought up with.

Jesus' journey to Gentile territory was a natural progression of His preaching the kingdom. We need to understand the deeply held religious beliefs of the day. Jews did not interact with Gentiles who, Jewish tradition taught, were considered "unclean" and "dogs". These beliefs do not disengage easily from them or us. In reading the parallel passage in Matt. 15:21-28, the disciples wanted to send the woman away (As we have seen, they often tried to send people away instead of addressing their issues).

In His encounter with the woman, Jesus let the twelve feel the shock of their own hidden prejudices and attitudes being spoken of and adopted by Jesus toward the Gentiles. He used this encounter to expose the disciples' exclusiveness and prejudices. Jesus' own attitude toward the woman and other Gentiles is seen by the outcome of the story.

The Bible is full of stories of God's grace and compassion extending to Gentiles. The promise was always to include all who came. The mission was to first present the gospel to the Jews so that they could be the purveyors or presenters of the truth. Their failure to take up the mantle was never a surprise to God, who always planned to include the Gentiles, (Isa. 42:6), but it was part of God's plan to give the Jews the first opportunity to bring the gospel to the whole world.

Upon their refusal, as Jesus just experienced in Mark 6-7, He moved on to Gentile territory with His message of inclusion. This is indeed good news for us!

Revelation reports that people from all tribes and nations will be present in heaven (Rev.7:9). Randy Alcorn in his book *Heaven* states that heaven itself will contain all the best of what every tribe and nation can offer from its culture.

Jesus then took the disciples full circle as they traveled back to Galilee where they were presented with a deaf and dumb man. With the Syrophoenician woman, Jesus didn't even have to speak to heal her daughter. Here, He actually shared His DNA with the man to make him well. As the crowds attested, "He has done all things well." And so He continues to do today, if we could but reach out and touch Him with faith.

Disciples' Perspective

Through their time with Jesus, the disciples faced a myriad of different experiences that they were not prepared for: Healing on the Sabbath; eating with unwashed hands; contact with lepers; casting out demons; being touched by unclean people; enduring violent storms in the night; placing truth over tradition; and finally, socializing with 'dogs'. They were face to face with their own prejudices and God's thoughts about them as they watched Jesus being confronted by a Gentile Greek woman. They were learning to see their own prejudices ("send the woman away") and observe that God is no respecter of persons.

As Jesus modeled for them, they were expected to break out of their own comfortable boxes and confront a whole new world – the world that God sees. He sees individuals in pain, up close and personal and He calls us to likewise keep our eyes open and see life from His perspective.

Historical Quote

"If we could read the secret history of our enemies, we should find in each man's life sorrow and suffering enough to disarm all hostility."
-Henry Wadsworth Longfellow

Getting to the Heart of the Matter

Today's Reading: Mark 7:24-37; parallel Passages: Matt. 15:21-31

Tyre and Sidon are northwest of Galilee on the shore of the Mediterranean Sea. In the Old Testament, it was known as Canaan – a place where Jews settled for some time. It was originally a pagan nation where many gods were worshipped. This could be one reason why the Jews of Jesus' day did not go there, and if they did, on their return they *shook off the dust* of the place from their shoes and clothes.

The Syrophoenician Woman
Read Mark 7:24-30

1. What facts do you see about the woman?

2. What do you learn about her daughter?

3. Read the parallel passage in Matt. 15:21-28 that speaks more of the disciples. What prejudices and traditions do you see from the disciples' statements about the woman?

4. How was Jesus' mission (stated in Mark 1:14-15) furthered by this encounter with the woman?

5. How did the woman's reaction to Jesus contrast with the Pharisees' reaction to Him as seen in prior lessons?

6. Do you think there is any significance to Mark's use of the word *little* three times? What does he call *little* in this passage?

The woman seemed to understand that by Jesus using the word first in Mark 7:27, He was leaving an opening to grant her request. Sometimes God leaves openings for our requests too. We think of them as maybes.

7. How did the woman follow up with Jesus on this? Should our response be similar when we get a maybe?

The woman seemed to be telling Jesus by her statements that He didn't have to interrupt His true mission to heal her daughter. He could quickly and easily fulfill her request and get back to teaching the disciples, but she made it clear that she was not leaving until He granted her request. Oh, to have such a faith!

8. Put yourself in the disciples' shoes in this passage. From what we have learned about being Jewish and their understanding of Gentiles, what prejudices might you expect to see surface? Now, think about your own life – what prejudices surface in your life about certain groups of people?

9. How did Jesus respond to the woman differently than the disciples might have?

The Deaf and Dumb Man
Read Mark 7:31-37

10. Write down the characteristics of the deaf and dumb man brought before Jesus.

11. Who brought the man to Jesus? What did they ask Jesus to do?

12. Read Mark 7:33-35. Write down everything Jesus did to the man.

13. Why do you think Jesus groaned or sighed as He was praying for the man?

14. Read Mark 7:37. The word for "utterly astonished" is a double imperative in the Greek and it means essentially, "above superabundance." Why do you think Mark used such an u

15. nusual phrase to record the people's response to what Jesus did?

> Mark 7:32 states that the man spoke with difficulty and could not be understood. The word used here in Greek is *mogilalos*, ("speech with difficulty") and its only use in the New Testament. The same word appears in the Septuagint (the Greek Old Testament) in Isa. 35:5-6, where it is God who comes to touch and heal. Some scholars believe this to be a prophetic fulfillment that the Messiah has come.

I don't know about you, but the Syrophoenician woman's faith puts mine to shame. Her love for her daughter is so strong and while she had probably only heard about Jesus, with no previous encounters, she is so firm and sure in her commitment. She "falls at His feet," argues with Him, and will not give up. She *knows* that He can cast out the demon from her daughter, and so sure is she that when He tells her to, "go your way," she goes home confident that her daughter was healed even though He had not spoken a word of healing or command.

She had the humility to know she deserved nothing, and the understanding of God's outrageous love to goad her in her determination to draw upon His bounteous grace! That's just the kind of person I'd like on my team, praying for me and beating down heaven's door for me and mine. And to think, like the disciples, we almost missed her. She was so different from the disciples. They couldn't see what Jesus saw. Who are we missing meeting up with due to our shortsightedness? Who should be in our lives but isn't because we lack the ability to see what Jesus saw?

Then too, I love the story of the healing of the deaf and blind man, don't you? I love how Jesus touches the man so intimately. He pulls the man aside, opens his ears so he can hear and then He frees the man's speech with His own saliva so the man can praise Him. It is not unlike what He does for you and me when we come to faith. He takes us out of the crowd, touches us with His own Spirit, opens our ears as we faithfully seek Him in His Word, frees our tongues to praise Him even as He frees our spirit from bondage. Oh what a Savior! Oh how He loves you and me.

Day 4
Do You Not See? More Sight-Seeing Lessons (Mark 8:1-26)

Personal Illustration: On Learning and Understanding

When our son was elementary school age we chose homeschooling. We used the *trivium method* of teaching which is based on a classical education theory. "Trivium" comes from the Latin word *tri* (three) and the Latin root *via* meaning road. The word literally means the "three-fold road or way."

Simply put, the learner goes through the learning process and the reading materials three times in their education, once for *knowledge*, once for *understanding* and once to learn how to *apply* what they've learned. By reading children's translations of the classics, he achieved a basic understanding of the book. For example, rather than reading *The Iliad and the Odyssey* in its adult translated version, he read the children's version. He gained knowledge about the classics and the stories became familiar to him, even though he hadn't read the actual originally translated version (which he wouldn't have been able to understand then).

Had he continued on in this method of teaching, he would read the actual books or the original documents (rather than reading someone's interpretation of them as is common in some textbooks today) as he moved from the knowledge stage to the understanding and application stage. Then he would learn to process the information and actually use what he learned as he began writing and speaking in his older years.

When he got to junior high we let him choose home-school or public school. Armed with a basic understanding of the classics he would read in high school and college, he chose public school.

Background Information

Although I don't think we can definitively say that Jesus used the trivium method to teach His disciples, in today's lesson we will be seeing some very familiar stories that we looked at in detail in Mark 6:31-7:37. Several scholars have noted a repetitive parallel structure in this section of Mark's gospel.

By just looking at the chart below, you can glean some of the lessons God considered important for the disciples to receive on multiple levels. As you review the chart, think about the repeated events listed. Why do you think they were significant enough for Mark to give them a subsequent pass-by for his readers?

First Encounter	Event	Second Encounter
6:31-44	Feeding of the multitude	8:1-9
6:45-56	Crossing of the sea and landing	8:10
7:1-23	Conflict with the Pharisees	8:11-13
7:24-30	Conversation about bread	8:14-21
7:31-36	Healing	8:22-26
7:37	Confession of faith	8:27-30

Rather than re-cycle through the information we've already learned, we will look at what Jesus did that was different, and what the disciples saw, heard and absorbed as they continued to learn from and observe Jesus.

Disciples Perspective

Sight is a common metaphor for understanding. The disciples, who at this point had been with Jesus a couple of years, should have had the beginnings of understanding of Who He is. They had knowledge but they didn't yet understand what they were seeing and hearing as Jesus moved through life with them at His side.

Nor did they understand how to apply what they saw happening in their own inner lives. They were still in the 'knowledge' phase of Jesus' teaching cycle. Though Jesus knew it, they weren't yet aware that they were on the road to Calvary. Just like we don't know what's ahead in our own lives, the disciples' faith and understanding needed to increase so they would have the necessary tools of faith to take them through what Jesus knew was in their future.

Historical Quote

"When God contemplates some great work, He begins it by the hand of some poor, weak human creature, to whom He afterwards gives aid, so that the enemies who seek to obstruct it are overcome."

-Martin Luther

Getting to the Heart of the Matter

Today's Reading: Mark 8:1-26
Parallel Passages: Matt. 15:32-39, Matt. 16:1-12

Feeding of the 4000

Read Mark 8:1-10.

1. **Why did Jesus share His compassion over the crowd's need with His disciples in Mark 8:1-3?**

2. **Mark 8:8 says the people ate and were satisfied. We all know what this means in a physical sense, but what about a spiritual sense? What does it mean to "eat and be satisfied" at Jesus' table?**

3. **What differences between this incident and Mark 6:31-44 do you see? What do you learn about the disciples from these two incidents?**

In Mark 6:31-44 Jesus met the need by *teaching the people.* In His compassion He saw that they were like sheep without a shepherd. The disciples called Jesus' attention to their lack of food and asked that the people be sent away. In Mark 8:1-10 Jesus' compassion for the people met the need by feeding them physically.

Here it is Jesus who called the disciples' attention to the lack of food. He recognized how important it was that the disciples understood the concept of feeding God's people (and not just physically).

Religious Leaders Ask for a Sign (Mark 8:11-13)
Read Mark 8:11-13

4. **Jesus had filled the land with infallible proofs or signs and miracles of various kinds. What kinds of miracles have we seen so far?**

5. **Why do you think the Pharisees didn't believe the miracles they had seen?**

6. **What do you think would have been enough for the Pharisees? What could Jesus have done differently that would cause them to believe?**

7. **What about today? Do you think people would believe if they saw a sign or miracle?**

8. **What do people need in order to believe today?**

9. **Think about this statement: "The gospel remains hidden by unbelief." How does this apply in this passage? What about today?**

> **Notice how Jesus uses everyday items to teach heavenly lessons. How can we incorporate this method into our own thinking?**

A Warning against False Teaching (Mark 8:14-21)
Read Mark 8:14-21.

10. **How many loaves of bread did the disciples have in the boat? Why do you think they were worried about this when they had twice seen Jesus provide bread for more than 9,000 people?**

11. **Read John 6:35. What did Jesus say about bread? What do you think it means?**

12. **What are some characteristics of yeast (the kind you make bread with)?**

Yeast in the culture of Jesus' day was understood by all groups to represent *corruption* or *evil* and some include *unbelief* as well. Hendriksen[35] held that the "yeast of the Pharisees" represented their *traditions* (see Mark 7); the "yeast of the Sadducees" represented their *skepticism* and the "yeast of Herod" represented *secularism*.

13. **Discuss briefly these three explanations for yeast and decide how they are present in society today. How does each "yeast" affect society today?**

    (a) The yeast of the Pharisees

    (b) The yeast of the Sadducees

    (c) The yeast of Herod

Jesus warned His followers against the infection of unbelief. Like yeast in dough, a lack of faith can permeate our lives until it breaks out into open rebellion against God.

14. **After reviewing Mark 8:17-18, what do you see in the disciples' conversation that might indicate the yeast of unbelief could be in them?**

15. **List the questions Jesus asked the disciples and their answers.**

16. **What did their answers reveal about their growth as disciples?**

17. **What stage of learning do their answers reveal they were in? (Refer to Background Information).**

---

[35] Hendriksen, IBID., 318

The Blind Man and Jesus (Mark 8:22-26)

Read Mark 8:22-26

18. **What was different about this particular healing than others we have seen in our study?**

19. **What are the stages of healing mentioned in this section? (See also 1 Cor. 13:12)**

20. **What three things happened to the man in Mark 8:25-26 when Jesus laid hands on him a second time.**

21. **When Jesus asked the man, "What do you see?" do you think it is significant that the first thing the man saw was a distorted view of people?**

22. **As you think about your own walk with Christ, how clearly do you see the people He came to die for? Is there a lesson for us in this story as to how we see people?**

23. **Do you think this was a parable (heavenly story) for how the disciples were seeing?**

I love how Jesus used everything to teach. In today's lesson He healed the blind man in stages, not only for the man, but for His disciples and for us. His method helps us to learn how to see and also to realize that sometimes healing takes time. When we come to Him we are blind, but Scripture tells us that wholeness is now within our grasp. Understanding begins to dawn. As we move forward in our Christian walk, we see dimly, like the blind man or the man Paul speaks of in 1 Cor. 13:12, "For now we see in a mirror dimly, but then face to face; now I know in part, but then I shall know fully just as I also have been fully known."

And what did the blind man see when he started to see more clearly? He saw people. The very heartbeat of Jesus is for the souls of men. He helps us to see people.

Through my experience with Women's Ministry at my former church, I came to love the women at that church so deeply sometimes it hurt. Every woman I came into contact with was my favorite. It was a privilege to pray for and love them. None of us were perfect or even close to perfect, but together we were a community of wounded healers, seeking communion with each other and seeking always to bring others alongside to love and be loved.

Jesus' words and works must be pondered and taken to heart, not forgotten. Dwelling on them prayerfully will increase faith, clear sight and enable us to see His desperate love for people and allow Him to live out His love for others through us. The healing by Christ of the blind man is a lesson to us to help us to bring His people into focus in our lives.

Day 5
Who Do You See That I Am? (Mark 8:27-38)

Background Information

This lesson takes us with Jesus and the disciples on the road to Caesarea Philippi where the disciples would face their 'final exam' on this part of the training. There is only one final exam question: "Who do you say that I am?" I chose to call this lesson, "Who Do You SEE That I am?" because our quest is not just to proclaim Him, but to see Him working in and around our lives.

Caesarea Philippi was a city located 25 miles north of the Sea of Galilee, home to numerous temples and religious worship sites. It was a pagan power center where Baal [a pagan god] and other pagan gods were openly worshiped in Old Testament times. At one point the town was named Panias after the god Pan (Greek word meaning *everything*). You may have heard of pantheism which means God is everything, everything is God, or the worship of everything.

Caesarea Philippi was located on a sheer granite cliff. Jesus, as the great parable-teller may have pointed to the adjacent cliffs when describing Peter as Petra or the *rock*. It was also the location of Peter's great awakening when he proclaimed Jesus as, "the Christ, Son of the *living* God" in contrast to the city that idolized every dead god.

Couched against the backdrop of the City of Rome on the one hand and Mt. Hermon (a metaphor for Israel's search for God) on the other, the road to Caesarea Philippi was a perfect backdrop for Jesus' question. With the splendor of man's highest achievements in Rome seen by Herod's palace, magnificent villas on hills, shrines and pagan temples, marketplaces and other accolades to man's achievement, Jesus confronted the disciples. Which will it be? As we consider today's parallels with its backdrop of wars, military valor, economic collapse, thirst for power, greed, the age of rising prices and rising princes, the question still remains the same: "Who do you say that I am?"

Disciples' Perspective

Today's lesson was not an easy one for the disciples nor will it be for us. In recognizing Who Jesus is, He called the disciples' to a deeper walk, one that would lead them to glory not through a reigning king but through a suffering servant. Jesus told believers that those who wished to follow Him must be prepared to shift the center of gravity in their lives from a concern for self to reckless abandon for the will of God. And so we begin to learn what it really means to be a disciple.

Historical Quote

"Christ calls men to carry a cross; we call them to have fun in His name. He calls them to forsake the world; we assure them that if they but accept Jesus the world is their oyster. He calls them to suffer; we call them to enjoy all the bourgeois comforts modern civilization affords...He calls them to holiness; we call them to a cheap and tawdry happiness that would have been rejected with scorn by the least of the Stoic philosophers." -A.W.Tozer

Getting to the Heart of the Matter

Today's Reading: Mark 8:27-38
Parallel Passages: Matt. 16:13-28, Luke 9:18-27, John 6:60-71

"Who Do You Say That I Am?", Mark 8:27-33
Read Mark 8:27-33.

1. **Review Mark 8:27-30 to find what questions Jesus asked the disciples and what answers were given to each question?**

2. **Why did Jesus warn the disciples to tell no one in Mark 8:30?**

Like the blind man who saw "men as trees walking" and saw only partially what he was meant to see, so Peter's confession of faith was given to him by God (see Matt. 16:17). But he and the disciples only partially saw the truth of what Peter was saying. Peter saw *something*, but he didn't really understand what he was seeing.

3. **Read Mark 8:31-33. What did Jesus teach them to expect in Mark 8:31?**

> **Out of his misguided love for Jesus, Peter the rock became Peter the stumbling block.**

4. In Mark 8:32, the word *rebuke* is the same word Jesus used in Mark 1 and 3 when rebuking demons. It was a strong word, one rarely used, but here Peter used it on his Teacher. Why do you think Peter used such a strong rebuke? Could Peter have been frightened of what Jesus' words in Mark 8:31 implied?

5. In Mark 8:31-33 Jesus presented a picture of the "Suffering Messiah". The Jews (including the disciples) rejected the idea of a suffering messiah as incompatible with their hopes and convictions. What do you think the disciples were hoping to hear? How do you respond?

Gather up what you've learned so far about Satan's tactics. So far we've seen him use the Pharisees, Jesus' family and we've even seen how Satan can use our friends to side-track us from God's will. Remembering these things helps us to see what is happening here.

6. Who was Jesus speaking to in Mark 8:33?

7. What did Jesus say?

8. What do you think it means?

9. When Jesus spoke to Satan through Peter, what was really going on here?

   (a) Is Jesus afraid? Tempted?

   (b) What does this tell you about Jesus' walk toward the Cross?

   (c) Does it give you any insight into your own walk?

The Cost of Discipleship (Mark 8:34-38)
Read 8:34-38.

Cross-bearing was a Roman custom used only for the vilest offenders in the community. It must have been quite distasteful to the Jews in the crowd. The disciples saw (sort of) Who Jesus is, but didn't recognize God's methods.

It is a common failing. We don't want to follow a suffering messiah either. We would much rather follow Him into resurrection without the death. We don't really want the Cross. We might want to consider the Cross, think on it, thank Him for it, but do we really want to share in it, partake of it or enter into it? But it is part of the call, isn't it? To follow where He leads. It is what surrender, sacrifice and self denial are all about. The disciples hadn't made the connection between suffering and serving leading to glory, but they were about to learn.

10. **In Mark 8:34 Jesus told His followers (the disciples and the multitudes) to do three things. List them, look at each one and come up with a one-word description for each concept.**

11. **Is there a difference between "self denial" and "denying self"?**

12. **In Mark 8:35-36 what three paradoxes are listed?**

Peter might have gotten part of the message, but he clearly missed out on the suffering part as seen by Jesus' rebuke. Through Peter's revelation the disciples were hopeful of setting up the kingdom – something they had suspicions and hopes about up to now. Kingdom yes, but not exactly the kingdom they were hoping for. They and other Jews were looking for a reigning messiah not a suffering messiah. This is not the kingdom of the glorious Messiah. This was not a road they wanted to go down.

13. **In Mark 8:36-37 Jesus talked about profit and loss. What do you gain (what is your profit) if you choose to follow Him whole-heartedly? What do you lose?**

14. **Review this chapter and jot down one or two concepts or principles that you think would help you as you live your life as a member of the kingdom.**

Profit and loss in terms of kingdom living is a difficult concept, isn't it? But I think the real question Jesus is asking His followers is whether we are willing to invest our lives in kingdom living or will we lose our lives (what we gain by kingdom living) for our own glory? It is a tough question to answer – one that takes us back to Tozer's quote at the beginning of this lesson. There is no second chance at kingdom living. While we might squeak by and still get into the kingdom, we will miss out on the true glory and great joy of living for Him in today's world in our own lives if we choose poorly at this crossroads in our walk with Him.

I think He is really saying that even if you gain the whole world, it's not enough to buy you a second chance at kingdom living. There is no greater answer to no greater question that you will ever answer than the one put before Peter: "Who do YOU say that I am?"

Perhaps you have never really answered that question adequately. Maybe you have muddled through this study so far wondering what it's all about, sensing, desiring, wanting more but not sure what it is. Let me just ask you bluntly: Have you ever acknowledged Jesus as *your* Savior? Have you acknowledged that His sacrifice on the cross was for *your* sin? If not, this may be the very moment, the very day of your salvation. Heb. 3:7-8 says, "Therefore, just as the Holy Spirit says, 'Today if you hear His voice, Do not harden your hearts…'" (NASB)

If His Spirit is calling you today, ask for His forgiveness; ask Him to become your Savior, give Him your life and your future. If you have done this with a heart yearning after God, it is done. Forevermore you are His child. To acknowledge this decision, place your name and the date below.

Date: _____

_____

Family Matters

You have choices this week. Either of the movies mentioned below would be excellent choices.

- *Fiddler on the Roof* – a touching, family-oriented movie with catchy music about a group of Russian Jews forced to leave their homes and disperse in early 19th century Russia. This movie has no hidden agenda, no message to plumb the depths -- just a bit of tradition from a time in history that has meaning for everyone. Tradition binds them with an invisible cord. Pay close attention to the song, *Tradition*.

- *Bonheoffer* -- a 2003 documentary about Dietrich Bonheoffer, a German pastor who spoke out about Nazi atrocities during WWII and was martyred for his faith. This hero of the faith illustrates "the cost of discipleship." Of the several movies of his life, this is my preference because it is so well done.

Looking Forward
Next Chapter: From the Heights to the Depths in our kingdom walk!

Chapter 6
From the Heights to the Depths (Mark 9-10)

Day 1
"Defining Moments" (Mark 9:1-13)

Personal Illustration

Several years ago I was driving down the street minding my own business. As I was preparing to get on the freeway I pulled up next to a car full of teenagers. I could hear their music blaring, interrupting my own quiet contemplation. I casually glanced over and, for a split second, saw the veil lift on their lives. I saw and felt all of the excruciating pain of their collective experiences and I felt a deep, overwhelming love for them.

I burst into uncontrollable sobs and had to pull over on the freeway because what I was experiencing was so painful. It was an extraordinary thing. Nothing like I had ever experienced before. It was as if, for a moment, I saw their lives through God's eyes. He pulled back the veil and I was able to feel the deeply intense, immense emotion God feels as He looks at us in love and sees where our choices may lead us.

The same thing happened one other time several months later a few hours before I was to speak at a women's retreat. The same wrenching pain, as, for a millisecond, the veil was thrown back on the lives of the women I was preparing to speak to. I saw the anguish in their lives, the agony some were feeling and the difficulties they were facing. I was left gasping when the moment flashed by.

That night I could hardly talk without weeping and I didn't know how to express what I had experienced. I couldn't really understand why I was given the vision or what it meant. Quite frankly, it still troubles me. But one thing I can say quite assuredly: The moments changed me. I thought about God and His love for me and others quite differently after that. It was no longer the sweet, sappy, cloudy kind of love I believed before. This was mind-boggling, gut-wrenching, gritty, powerful, wild love. And it hurt. It was something to be experienced not explained.

I share this story here because it reminds me of what Peter, James and John may have experienced on the mountain with Jesus in Mark 9:1-13. For them, as for me, it was a defining moment. A *defining moment* has been characterized as an occurrence that typifies or determines all related events that follow. We've all had some: birth of a child (that certainly changes things!); becoming a Christ-follower; weddings; divorces; death of a loved one; or just those moment-in-time words sometimes offered sincerely, sometimes in passing: *You have a gift for helping people. You impacted my family when you brought a meal. You need to write.*

Then there are the spiritual defining moments that take more sight and insight. The moments when we *know* God has spoken into our lives: circumstances come together to answer our prayer in a definite way; people meet a need without knowing it existed; God moves on to our path and we *see* Him.

Peter, James and John experienced a blinding moment when they saw Jesus and heard the Voice of God speaking to them from the cloud. Defining moments change us.

Background Information

The Christian life is a series of paradoxes. To become great we must become a servant (Mark 9:33-37); to stand tall, we stoop to welcome (Mark 9:36-37); to protect truth, we allow others to speak (Mark 9:38-41); to worship, we accept suffering (Mark 9:49). In this study Jesus took Peter, James and John with Him to pray on Mount Hermon. There they experienced a life-changing event, the ramifications of which they had little understanding at the time.

When they returned, they found the other disciples in the midst of a confrontation they were unable to handle and heard a father's cry for help which in reality was a prayer for faith. This compelled Jesus to act. Finally the disciples questioned Jesus on the meaning of greatness. His answer was not one they desired to hear nor implement.

We are also given a glimpse into the afterlife from this passage. As Jesus and the disciples met with Moses and Elijah (who had been dead for hundreds of years), we learn several things: Their presence with Jesus bore witness to life after death; Moses and Elijah were recognizable to Jesus and the disciples, and also presumably to each other. God spoke so others could hear. The command to, "Listen to My Son" gave specific, detailed and clear direction for kingdom living.

Disciples' Perspective

What happened to Jesus on the mountain is symbolic of what He wanted to do in the lives of the disciples (and ours). He wants to teach us how to bring the mountain-top into the valley where we live every day. Lloyd Ogilvie said, "When we are in touch with the dynamic and creative energy which created the world and became incarnated love in Jesus, we are transfigured by the glory of God."[36]

---

[36] Ogilvie, IBID.

It is God's great desire for us to listen to His Son because He knows therein lies true greatness and the power to transform our lives and others.

Historical Quote

"You are writing a gospel, a chapter each day; By deeds that you do, by words that you say. Men read what you write, whether faithless or true. Say, what is the gospel according to you?" John R. Rice, Quoted in *Poems that Preach*

> To the Jewish mind and understanding of Scripture God meets people on mountain tops. Moses and Elijah met God there; Abraham went to a mountain top to sacrifice his son Isaac and met the God Who, "provided Himself, the sacrifice" instead. God can and does meet us anywhere and everywhere.

Getting to the Heart of the Matter

Passage: Mark 9:1-13
Parallel passages: 2 Pet. 1:16-18; Matt. 17:1-13; Luke 9:28-36

If you have never looked at the painting of *The Transfiguration* by Raphael, I urge you to take a minute to look it up now if you have access to a computer. You will find it an amazing study in itself.

Three levels of awareness and activity are shown in the painting. First, at the top of the painting we see Jesus, Moses and Elijah in the heavenly realm conversing about things to come, while in the second level the three disciples are waking up from sleep and looking in wonder at Jesus and His visitors. On the third level life was going forward in the lives of those on earth below.

The remaining nine disciples are in one place arguing with the scribes while a desperate father helplessly watches his demon-possessed son suffering in agony. No one seems able or willing to help him. Some of the spectators appear to be pointing upward toward the heavens as if to say Jesus is the boy's only hope. It opens the mind to a whole host of possibilities, doesn't it? It gives me hope and reminds me that I'm not alone.

Mark 9:1-13

Transfiguration is a *visual* depiction of Peter's spoken word in Mark 8:27. The Greek word for 'transfigure' is *metamorphoomai*. It means *to change form* (same word in Rom. 12:1, 2 Cor. 3:18).

1. **Who is present on the mountain? (Hint: there are seven persons present.)**

2. **Read the parallel passage in Luke 9:28-36. What do you learn from Luke that is not mentioned in Mark?**

3. **Read the Mark (9:1-13) passage and list the events in order as they occur. Write down what the three disciples with Jesus saw and heard.**

4. **Read Luke 9:30-31. What were Jesus, Elijah and Moses talking about?**

The phrase in Luke 9:31, "they were speaking of His departure which He was about to accomplish" is an odd way of speaking of death. The word used for *death* in these verses is *decease* which means *exodus*. They spoke of the exodus Jesus was about to accomplish. Moses led an exodus of the people from Egypt and Elijah led a kind of exodus of the people from apostasy and idolatry. (1Kings 18:16-39) But Jesus was to accomplish both an exodus for all redeemed people from sin's bondage, and from death.

5. **Some skeptics have downplayed the transfiguration as a vision or a dream but not a real event. It was real to Peter. Compare this idea with 2 Pet. 1:16-18 and Mark 9:9. What do you think? And, does it matter?**

6. **It is interesting that it is Moses (lawgiver) and Elijah (prophet) who are on the mountain giving homage to Jesus. Jesus came as the fulfillment of both the Law and the prophets. Read Romans 10:4 and Acts 10:43. What do the verses say about Jesus' mission?**

We can learn much about heaven or the afterlife from this passage. Think about these points:

- Moses and Elijah were alive as *individuals*
- They did not have wings (and humans do not become angels after death)
- They were recognizable personalities (recognized by the disciples)
- They were conscious (not soul sleeping)
- Their bodies were glorified – similar but different to ours in that they could disappear and appear
- They enjoyed community, talking with Jesus and each other
- They appeared to be aware of what was happening on earth (they spoke with Jesus about His coming death).

7. **What else do you see in this passage about life after death?**

8. **Do you think this event had a lasting impact (or was a "defining moment") on the three disciples? Why?**

9. **What elements of worship do you see here?**

We worship the only way we know how until God draws us deeper in. For me, in the beginning of my walk, worship was singing in church and maybe singing hymns on a hillside around a campfire with my friends. As I grew in my walk worship became increasingly broader. Soon it was taking a meal to a sick or hurting family or writing a note to a discouraged friend; it was teaching a Bible Study or speaking at a retreat. Worship is anything we do or offer up unreservedly to Him.

10. **How did Peter worship in this passage? How did Peter define worship in 2 Pet. 1:16-18?**

11. **Write the words God used when He spoke from the cloud.**

> **Obedience and discipleship come together in Mark 9:7 as the three heard the actual command of God's Voice to *listen to Jesus*. Suddenly Mark 8:27 has a new meaning. While the command in Mark 1:17 to "follow Me" was the beginning, as we walk deeper and continue to follow, the more intimate call is to "listen to Me."**

Transfiguration is an event that may be experienced but not usually explained. It is about knowing Christ and going from a proclamation of truth in our lives that we hardly understand ("You are the Christ; Son of the living God") to a living, active, life-changing discovery of the living God in our midst. It is where blindness gives way to discovery and from there to insight. Our defining moments, like Peter, make up the core of our faith as we learn to see and encounter Him in new and increasingly more personal ways.

Transfiguration is also about learning to worship. Peter's statement, "We will make a tabernacle," showed how Peter understood worship. For us, it is learning to live out Romans 12:1-2, ("Present your bodies as a *living sacrifice*") where the Father takes our living sacrifice and transforms us from the inside out. And everything that we do for Him that follows is a result of the transformation.

The passage about the transfiguration speaks to our own depth of prayer and worship. God uses the ordinary in our lives to reveal the extraordinary. Jesus reveals Himself in the transfiguration glory whenever someone receives insight and trusts or exercises faith. I want to be a living sacrifice of God's movement in and through my life every day. I want others to see Him, not me as I serve. I desire for you and me to *see* Him working as we learn to go from sight to insight in our walk of faith.

Day 2
The Paradox of Prayer and Unbelief (Mark 9:14-32)

Background Information

One thing we can always know about Jesus was that He always kept "the main thing the main thing." Theological debate was not (and still is not) usually on His agenda. When He arrived on the scene of today's study with Peter, James and John, His discussion with the three disciples after the transfiguration was finished.

He ignored the scribes and ended their bullying of the other disciples who were oblivious to the life and death drama going around them. He asked one question, then focused right in on what was important: People in pain. Here was a young son suffering with what is generally accepted by scholars and physicians alike to have been a form of epilepsy. The disease was made worse by a demon who took hold of the boy, striking him deaf and mute, terrorizing the young man almost to death right in front of Jesus. The father explained that he had these terrifying fits often.

With razor sharp intuition, Jesus centered on the one thing hindering the situation that would change everything: *Unbelief.* It is what locks away the power in any situation into which God is invited. Unbelief was present in every corner of today's study:

- The disciples lacked the power to cast the demon out of the young man. They failed to exercise their faith through prayer, even though time after time they saw Jesus with hands raised toward heaven in supplication and prayer.

- The scribes lacked compassion and were more interested in plaguing the disciples while Jesus was gone than in helping a hurting soul. They had no belief at all in Jesus' ability to touch and heal.

- In one statement Jesus turned the tables on the father and changed everything: "All things are possible to him who believes." Jesus provided the conduit or channel for the power of God to be evident, and prayer was the remedy. The disciples had the resources and the power but they didn't understand or know how to use what they had been given. The father on the other hand, immediately saw his opportunity when Jesus spoke, and uttered the most heart-felt, time-honored, oft-answered prayer in history: "I do believe. Help me in my unbelief."

Disciples' Perspective

While Jesus and the three disciples were coming down from the mountain, the remaining nine were embroiled in a discussion or dispute with the scribes while off to the side a desperate father unsuccessfully sought their help for his demon-possessed son. They had the authority but they lacked the faith. Hmm. Sound familiar?

They knew the remedy (prayer) but their attitude of unbelief and self-confidence based on past successes made them powerless. Their previous experiences with expelling demons did them no good in the present situation. That is because, like manna, His power must be continually sought and daily asked for. Radical reliance on His power alone was what was missing from their lives. And, while I hate to be so needy, I confess it is often missing from my life as well.

Historical Quote

"Too often we settle for much less than what God wants to do through us…Moses would have readily acknowledged his belief in God's power; he simply did not believe God could do His miraculous work through *his* life." -- Henry Blackaby[37]

Getting to the Heart of the Matter

Today's Reading: Mark 9:14-32
Parallel Passages: Matt. 17:14-23, Luke 9:37-45

Today we are going to look at the same passage from three different perspectives. First, we will review the passage from the disciples' perspective, then from Jesus' perspective and finally, from the boy's father's perspective. This will help us develop the skill of being able to see things from a different vantage point. It is a useful skill in life to be able to look at situations from a viewpoint different than our own. Before you begin, make a list of who is present in today's section of Scripture.

From the Disciples Perspective (Mark 9:14-32)

Review Mark 9:14-32.

1. **In Mark 9:16, what is the question Jesus asked? Who answered the question?**

2. **In Mark 9:17-18, why do you think the disciples could not cast out the demon from the boy?**

---

[37] Henry Blackaby and Richard Blackaby, *Experiencing God Day by Day*, (Nashville: Broadman & Holman, 1998).

3. What does this passage say about where the power comes from to live in the Spirit? Do you think this is still true today?

4. Review Mark 9:28-29. What question was asked by the disciples and what answer did Jesus give?

5. How do we incorporate what Jesus told the disciples in Mark 9:29 into our lives today?

6. Review Mark 6:7-13 concerning the authority given to the disciples. What do you think is different between the power they were given then and what was lacking here.

7. Were they trusting in themselves or God?

8. What hindered them?

9. What lessons do you learn from the passage for your life today?

From Jesus' Perspective (Mark 9:14-32)

Review this section of Scripture again, this time from Jesus' point-of-view.

10. What did Jesus see when He returned from the mountain?

11. Where was His focus?

12. How did He lead the boy's father in describing the situation?

13. What lessons do you see in how Jesus relates to people in crisis?

14. Review the passage and list the questions Jesus asked and the answers given. What do the answers show you about how God works?

From the Boy's Father's Perspective (Mark 9:14-32)

Review this again, this time from the point-of-view of the boy's father.

15. "Help me in my unbelief," is one of the most amazing prayers in the Bible. Can you remember a situation in your life when you prayed this prayer?

16. Discuss the connection between *faith* and *power to heal* as seen in this portion of Scripture. Write down any thoughts you have on this subject.

17. Do you think the disciples' inability to help the man's son had anything to do with his doubt as to Jesus' power?

It wasn't only the boy who needed healing, but the father's flagging hope needed a dose of regeneration too. Jesus did not disappoint. The rally cry of Jesus as He questioned the man is, "If you can! But don't you know – all things are possible if you believe." This engendered an immediate prayer response in the father: "I do believe! Help me in my unbelief." As my own faith sags, I pray it too. I want to be honest about my doubting and my own unbelief. *I never, never, never want my faith (or lack thereof) to be a source of disappointment in others' lives!*

18. Look at Jesus' response to the father's comment, "…if you can." What is the difference between "if you can" and "if you will"? What does this verse show about the father's faith or lack of it?

19. Compare Mark 9:22 ("if you can") with Mark 1:40-42 ("if you will") What differences do you see between the two passages?

20. In Mark 9:29, what is the connection between faith and prayer?

21. Which do you struggle with the most? Believing Jesus *can* or believing Jesus *will?*

This lesson brings up a lot of unanswered questions in my life and perhaps yours too. The connection between my faith and God's power is a scary one. What if my faith isn't enough? What if my lack of faith causes someone to stumble, like the disciples in this chapter? What if someone can't be healed because I don't believe enough? What if, like the desperate father whose fledgling faith hung in the balance between his son's healing and lack thereof, I fail to cry out in my unbelief for the constancy of continued belief? The enemy of our souls can place an anchor around questions like this that will sink us if we don't stay focused on our Champion.

There are times when we pray, pray and pray. Thousands of people may pray with us and someone still isn't healed. What then? What about those times when we *really believe* God is going to heal and He doesn't? What then? Is it my fault that someone dies? Have I failed someone I really love because my faith wasn't enough? Am I like the disciples? Believe me when I say that these important questions can sink us if we misunderstand what the Scripture is saying in passages like the one we've studied today.

To understand, we need to go back to the mountaintop of Transfiguration. What happened to Jesus there is symbolic of what He wants for each of His children. To bring the mountain into the valley below where faith falters and disease and demons predominate. He wants us to be sure of His presence and guidance in our lives as we walk in the valley; to understand our need to be with Him more than our need to be with others; to trust His heart when we can't trace His hand. It is only as we put our faith and trust in Him to do the work that things happen.

Our job is to follow where He leads, pray as He directs and leave Him to answer according to His will. Pray in faith? Yes. Pray without doubting? Yes. But trust in His sovereignty and leave the outcome to Him. William Lane says, "When faith confronts the demonic [or any other situation], God's omnipotence is its sole assurance and God's Sovereignty is its only restriction."[38]

Today we have seen the principle of faith set free. When freed from doubt and in the belief that *God Can*, power is released. Through our own awareness, we cannot solve the problem, but God CAN. It is only when we understand this principle that faith is free to move.

Can you trust Him today? Can you trust Him when the answer is not the one you asked for? Can you move out from your pain and fear, your deep-seated, wrongly held beliefs that maybe He can, but He probably won't; or maybe He won't but He probably can – and put your situation into His Hands? It is the only way to build faith out of broken dreams, unbelief and impaired vision. He is a God who

---

[38] Lane, IBID., 333

can be trusted with our most desperate heart-cries. *"And I will never leave you or forsake you."* (Hebrews 13:5)

Day 3
Preparing for the Unexpected (Mark 9:30-50)

Background Information

Just this morning my husband and I were faced with a daunting decision: do the right thing and face months, maybe years of suffering and hardship or take the easy way out and let things go, taking the hit and moving on with our lives. It's a difficult decision isn't it? Sometimes the best thing is to "let it go and move on." But sometimes, when a just outcome is at stake, win or lose, we must choose the harder path. There have been many, many times when I have counseled clients and taken the advice myself to move on – let justice go and expect that God will have His vengeance (Rom. 13:19).

But there have also been times when I have had to stand on my own, take the hit, pay the consequence and suffer the hardship because it is *the right thing to do*. So, this morning I woke up with a pain in my gut over the thought of the future and offered a fervent prayer for mercy. And God showed up. He didn't miraculously solve the problem, but He spoke.

In my daily reading I came to Exodus 3. I knew what was coming as I had passed through this section of Scripture many times before. But, as my husband always says, "The miracle is in the timing." As I read about Moses' encounter with the burning bush, as he stood shoeless and clueless before God, I read God's words to Moses: "I have *seen* the affliction of my people; I have *heard* their cries; I am *aware* of their sufferings; so *I have come down* to deliver them…and I am sending *you.*" And they became God's words to me. He has seen, He has heard, He is aware of our sufferings, He will deliver and He will come down to work through people like Moses, and sometimes me and you. The assurance that I am not alone in this battle, and that He is a God *who sees* is all I needed to pull myself up out of the pit and get moving.

Disciples' Perspective

By now the disciples should be "getting it," we think. I wonder sometimes if they aren't suffering from willful blindness. I do that sometimes when I don't want to face what's coming. Like this morning's dilemma. I'd rather put my head in the sand and pretend it doesn't exist. But Jesus is always speaking into our lives and whether we are afraid to ask for clarification, we really do not understand, (Mark

9:32) or we just don't hear, does not change the truth of His words spoken into our lives.

There is no more important task than for us to listen for His Voice and to do what He asks of us at this very moment. The disciples are churning and yearning for something they can't even communicate – something they don't *think* they want, but history shows us that on moving forward for Christ, their lives would count for eternity and they would be satisfied in the giving.

Historical Quote
"When I pray, coincidences happen and when I do not pray, they do not happen."
-William Temple, late Archbishop of Canterbury.

Getting to the Heart of the Matter

Today's Reading: Mark 9:30-50
Parallel Passages: Matt. 18:1-9, Luke 9:46-50

Teachings on Death and Resurrection (Mark 9:30-32)
This section contains an interesting concept that we miss by not understanding Jewish culture and theology. The phrase "delivered up" is actually a concept that finds roots in Jewish theology on martyrdom. It doesn't mean a person just unfortunately comes under someone's power by being in the wrong place at the wrong time – it is a phrase meaning an "actual fulfillment of God's will." It is God who permits or protects someone from being "handed over" to fulfill His deeper purposes. It speaks to God's Sovereignty. The disciples heard this but couldn't understand why God would permit His Son, Messiah, King to be handed over to mere men. They didn't see what Jesus was telling them all along - that God's plan was to give up His Son to buy back humanity from the enemy. It was the only way to effect a rescue. (Recall our analysis of Mark 3:27 and how to rescue someone from enemy territory.)

Read Mark 9:30-32.

1. **What three things was Jesus teaching the disciples?**

2. **How did they respond to what they heard?**

3. **Why were the disciples afraid to ask Jesus to explain His comments?**

Teachings on Greatness in the Kingdom (Mark 9:33-37)

Read Mark 9:33-37

4. How did Jesus define *greatness* in this passage?

> In the Aramaic language, the word for *child* is the same word used for *servant.*

5. What principles for Christian living do you see in His definition?

6. Read Proverbs 16:18. Do you think this verse has any bearing to this passage?

7. What do you think Jesus meant when He described greatness in terms of the *least?*

8. What do you see as connection between faith and greatness?

9. Jesus used the visual aid of a child to give the disciples a parable or story about greatness. What qualities do you see in children that might have caused Jesus to set them up as an example of living?

Teachings on Following Christ (Mark 9:38-41)

The irony here is that at this point the disciples themselves had been powerless in a situation involving exorcism and now they were criticizing someone else successfully employing it in Christ's Name. Read the section Mark 9:38-41.

10. Do you think this shows a "narrow perspective" of the work of God or is there some truth to it?

11. Jesus seemed to think the man in this passage was the real deal. Is there any way to distinguish a charlatan from a true follower of Christ? Review Acts 19:13-16, Matt. 7:21-23, Num. 11:27-29 for some help.

12. **What was Jesus' perspective here? What attitudes and actions should govern our relationship with groups that act in Jesus' Name but worship or serve differently?**

Teachings on Radical Discipleship (Mark 9:41-48)

This section is not a demand by Jesus that we cut off our hand, pluck out our eye or lop off our feet, but is a picture of the radical nature of how to treat sin when it creeps in or boldly takes over our lives. When exposed, sin must be dealt with radically and immediately. Jesus was telling His disciples to put all habits, sins and practices under submission to kingdom living. Whatever gets in the way of your relationship with Christ, cut it off and cast it out. Be vigilant, focused and sober.

We all have them: sins, habits, practices. If we can name them, they are easier to deal with. If we can't name them, we should pray for God to expose them.

13. **What sins, habits or practices in your life make obedience and faithfulness to Christ difficult?**

14. **In this section, Jesus, the only Person in the New Testament Who talked about hell, mentioned it three times (though some scholars point out that Mark 9:44 and :46 are not in the best ancient manuscripts). How does Jesus describe hell in these verses?**

Gehenna, translated *hell*, was a real place outside the city of Jerusalem where garbage was continually burned 24 hours a day. It was the place where dead carcasses were thrown, together with all of the waste of the city. It was also the place where Ahaz and Manasseh made child sacrifices to the foreign god Molech in 2 Kings 16:3-4.

Teachings on Salt (Mark 9:49-50)

As background read Rom. 12:1-2 and Rev. 2:13.

15. **To be "salted with fire" refers to being purified for God. What do you think this means? How does this process happen in our lives?**

16. **What characteristics of salt could Jesus be referring to in Mark 9:50? What does it have to do with discipleship?**

In today's lesson amidst warnings, teachings and attempts by Jesus to communicate what was coming, He wanted His disciples to understand the true meaning of the upside down, inverted, against-the-grain lifestyle they would pursue if they remained with Him.

Through the paradoxes of suffering leading to glory, leadership identified by serving, and following touched by continual challenges and hardship, Jesus taught, modeled, mentored and prepared His disciples to face the Via Dolorosa.[39]

The lessons have not changed. Jesus still wants to communicate His path for our lives. Remember the Father's command, "Listen to My Son" and be changed.

Day 4
Telling the Hard Truth (Mark 10:1-31)

Personal Illustration

I was single for what seemed like a very long time. I was in fourteen weddings before my own and was a "maid of honor" five times before marriage and twice after. That represents a lot of good friends moving on with their lives while I perceived mine was going nowhere because I wasn't married. I found it difficult to go to church alone; and when I did go, they didn't know what to do with me if they saw me at all. I knew *who* I wanted to marry; however, my beloved and I did not see eye to eye on the subject for a period of years. Happily, he eventually moved over from the "dark side" and I've been thanking God for him ever since.

I haven't been divorced, but I have been alone and I have often felt as though I failed in some way or another because of it.

One of the topics we tackle today is one I wish was in another gospel, but we committed at the beginning of this study not to turn aside from Jesus' hard sayings but to face them head on. Today, Jesus speaks of divorce. Some of you doing this study have troubled marriages; others have marriages that have ended in divorce with all of the guilt and pain that comes with it; still others are single or remarried. Remember that God takes us just as we are, right where we are and fills our lives with grace to move into His kingdom. He will use our failures our triumphs and even our sin to teach us and move us.

Background Information

In beginning this section, I could feel the inner lawyer in me gearing up for argument. The Pharisees tracked Jesus down as He proceeded with the disciples

---

[39] Spanish for 'The Road of Suffering'

toward Jerusalem and attempted to engage Him in the question of, "When is it lawful for a man to divorce a wife?" (Mark 10:2)

It will help us in reading this section if we understand the thinking of the day. It was, like today, a very controversial issue in the religious community and also in Rome. (Recall Mark is writing to Roman believers). History reports that Rome began to recognize a woman's right to divorce her husband as early as 50 B.C., though a woman's right was only allowed by Jewish Law in rare instances.[40] However, several scholars agree that, "On the question of the lawfulness of divorce, there was general unanimity among the Jews: divorce was allowed."[41]

The Pharisees were not so interested in what Jesus actually thought about the matter as they were in trying to trap Him. There was no way Jesus could have pleased everyone because there were two schools of thought on the issue stated in the Mosaic Law at Deut. 24:1-2. One group's thinking came from the popular teacher of the day, Rabbi Shammai, who interpreted the passage as more restrictive, advising his students that the *only* reason a man could divorce his wife was for sexual unfaithfulness; while the other teacher, Rabbi Hillel, had a more generous interpretation of the verses. Hillel told his students that whatever irritated a husband in a marriage was grounds for divorce. In other words, "any reason" was acceptable, more like today's divorce laws.

I don't plan to jump into the middle of this discussion with my opinions and neither did Jesus. He told them God's intentions regarding marriage, turning the subject away from divorce. He explained the principles of marriage rather than the concession in the Mosaic Law. He told them that divorce was a violation of God's ideal and left it to them to figure it out, though He did speak with His disciples more stringently on the issue.

Jesus kept His focus on kingdom living, and had other lessons for the disciples. In today's lesson He rebuked the disciples for forbidding children to come to Him. He confronted a young man who preferred to trust in his wealth rather than kingdom living. Ever a Gentleman God, He felt the sorrow and pain of the man's monumental decision but did not seek to change his mind.

Disciples' Perspective

If the disciples weren't so woefully descriptive of me, I might begin to feel a bit irritated with their obtuseness. But they, like me, were children of their culture. They were students of Mosaic Law to some degree and probably believed in one of the two schools of thought of the day on divorce.

---

[40] Lane, IBID., 358.
[41] Hendriksen, IBID., 710.

They probably also bought into the culture which did not hold children in high regard and glorified the wealthy as holding the favor of God. When Jesus continually turned their thinking upside down, it was understandably difficult to grasp. This is the very heart of kingdom living – learning to see things from God's perspective: God views marriage as the ideal, allowing divorce because of our inability to see. He holds children in high regard because they know how to receive without suspicion. He feels compassion for the wealthy who depend on their supply rather than a Savior, but is never moved to create exceptions for people in how to find Him.

Historical Quote

"...any unwillingness to deal graciously with human failure is a telltale sign of unforgiven regions in us." - Lloyd Ogilvie

> Marriage is God's ideal. "God joins a couple together. This was the original intention of the Creator. Any violation of this is sin, but it is not the unpardonable sin..." – J. Vernon McGee

Getting to the Heart of the Matter

Today's Reading: Mark 10:1-27
Parallel Passages: Matt. 19:3-30, Luke 16:18, Luke 18:15-30

The Pharisees Question Jesus about Divorce (Mark 10:1-12)

Recall that the gospel of Mark was written with Roman believers in mind, many of whom were not familiar with Mosaic Law.

1. **The Pharisees attempted to trap Jesus by their questions. In Mark 10:2 they were "testing Him" (other manuscripts read they were "tempting Him"). John the Baptist was beheaded for speaking out on the subject. Perhaps, they reasoned, if Jesus spoke out, Herod would hear of it and arrest Him too. No matter what Jesus said about this controversial topic, someone would be dissatisfied. What do you think the Pharisees' really wanted from Jesus here? See J. Vernon McGee's comment on this portion of Scripture in sidebar.42**

2. **Read Deut. 24:1-2. What does the passage say about divorce?**

3. **How did Jesus respond to the Pharisees' questions?**

4. **How did Jesus explain Deut. 24:1-2? Why do you think this law was enacted?**

---

42 J. Vernon McGee, *Thru the Bible with J. Vernon McGee, Vol IV Matthew-Romans,* (Grand Rapids:Thomas Nelson 1983), 203.

The Call to Follow Jesus

5. What was God's purpose for marriage *from the beginning*? (Mark 10:6-9)

6. In Mark 10:11-12, how was Jesus' discussion with the disciples different from His discussion with the Pharisees?

Jesus Blesses the Little Children (Mark 10:13-16)
Read Mark 10:13-16

7. Why did people bring their children to Jesus? (Mark 10:13)

8. How were the disciples' actions in Mark 10:13 different than Mark 9:38? What lessons, if any, were they missing?

9. What do you think Jesus meant when He said that the kingdom of God belongs to such as these (children)?

10. Since this study in large part focuses on kingdom living, what Jesus said in this section is important. How does being like a child prepare you or help you understand kingdom living better or differently?

11. How do you receive the kingdom of God like a child?

12. Do you see any significance to the fact that the concepts in Mark 10:1-13 and Mark 10:14-16 are back-to-back?

The Greek word for *blessing* in this passage is *katalogein* which means to "bless fervently." Do you ask God to bless you fervently? What would such a blessing look like in your life? It may give clues to what you consider important.

Plight of the Wealthy (Mark 10:17-27)
It was commonly assumed in Jesus' day (like today) that the wealthy were especially favored by God since He controls wealth. Jesus turned the assumption upside down by telling His disciples how hard it is for the rich to enter the kingdom of heaven. He didn't say they could not enter, only that it was more

difficult. Jesus never condemned people for being rich but He discerned in the young man of today's story as being powerfully connected to his possessions.

We have a very good friend who is quite well off but she has no trouble with kingdom living because she depends solely on the Lord for His provision in her life. She is quiet, unpretentious, generous and can be trusted with wealth because she can handle it without it handling her. Our bank account on the other hand, usually stays pretty close to empty. I suspect it is because God cannot yet trust us to depend on Him for our resources. I don't mean to be flippant, but there are times when I would like to give it a try nonetheless.

13. **Why did the young man call Jesus good in Mark 10:17?**

14. **What did Jesus' reply in Mark 10:18 mean?**

15. **According to Mark 10:21, what was the one thing the young man lacked in his spirituality?**

By using the word *inherit* in Mark 10:17, there is an implication of deserving. The young ruler may have thought he deserved entrance to the kingdom because of his deeds and even his wealth. But Jesus never changes the requirements for entrance. He never moves the bar into a sliding scale just so some can enter. It is always and ever the same – putting faith and trust in Jesus is the only way. It wasn't the man's wealth that kept him out of the kingdom, but his unwillingness to let it go for Christ's sake. What he owned, owned him.

16. **Why do you think the young man could not comply with Jesus' request? (Mark 10:22)**

17. **What was the one thing the young man lacked that was necessary for him to enter into kingdom living?**

18. **Why were the disciples amazed at Jesus' words in Mark 10:23?**

19. **Read Mark 10:29-31. What did Jesus promise those who choose to live in His kingdom?**

One problem with expository study is dealing with difficult passages in Scripture as in today's study on divorce. We will not solve the divorce question for everyone. Thousands of books and sermons have addressed this topic without definitively solving it in today's culture.

If this is a topic that in some way touches you, prayerfully seek God's guidance as you study the words of Jesus. As believers we don't have the luxury of picking and choosing favorite truths. They are what they are. God's blessings don't stop, His love never changes toward us when we do not do everything we are commanded to do, but our choices matter. As we have already learned throughout this study, our choices may bring consequences we would rather not experience or would not wish our loved ones to face. Also, sometimes it is not us but others' poor choices which impact us and we suffer because someone else's sin touched us.

Nor can we always grasp kingdom living as Jesus taught His disciples. They, like us, have difficulty tracking not only what Jesus told them, but how to live it out. But we know the end of the story, like the young pastor's story in Chapter Three, Day Three. The disciples rocked the world and started a revolution that continues to this day.

Because they stayed the course, pursued the kingdom and followed the King, we can know Him today. I don't know about you but I'm grateful to those who over the centuries have not given up and pushed through to know God deeper. Because of them, I too can know Him and grow deeper. We need each other.

Day 5
On the Road to Jerusalem (Mark 10:32-52)

Background Information

As the time of Passover neared many were on the road to Jerusalem and undoubtedly fell in behind Jesus and the disciples. Jesus alone knew what would happen there. He tried to warn His disciples but for whatever reasons, they were not hearing. Thus, in the following chapters, we will see pictures of Jesus' aloneness in the journey. Rather than walking at His side, the disciples and others followed behind Him as He walked on ahead (Mark 10:32).

His teaching methods were the same but people were less inclined to hear or understand Him, with a few notable exceptions. As the disciples squabbled over who would be the greatest in the kingdom (which they believed was imminent), Jesus, for the third time, explained what was coming. His sympathy for what they would encounter did not lessen yet He continued to expose kingdom living as an inverted lifestyle, upsetting the normal way of things by connecting glory and suffering, defining greatness as servant-hood and communicating what awaited "those who wish to be first."

Jesus set a new spiritual pace on the way to Jerusalem and the disciples were finding it more taxing to keep up. As we will see in future studies, the closer Jesus got to Golgotha, the further the disciples lagged behind. Their knowledge of Who Jesus is and what His purpose in coming would be had not yet reached their hearts.

As they approached Jericho, about fifteen miles from Jerusalem, they passed many beggars on the roadside. There is no record that Jesus healed everyone He passed or saw, but there are those whose exercise of faith often caught His attention. When blind Bartimaeus ("Son of Honor") heard that Jesus was passing by, He called out in a desperate plea for mercy. His cry was a bringing together of mercy and Messiahship[43], displaying a profound discernment that even the disciples lacked. When he was told by the crowd to be quiet, he cried out even more, requesting an audience with the One and Only.

When Jesus called for him, just like the many others who have been touched by Jesus, his life is changed in an instant. But consider that Jesus' life might also have been touched. Being surrounded by disciples who can't see, in restoring sight to one who CAN see, Jesus' own purpose is restored.

Disciples' Perspective

The disciples were not at their best in today's lesson. There was infighting, selfishness, scrabbling for position, un-teachable spirits, pride, arrogance and a host of other maladies that plague the human spirit. Kingdom living is always an uphill walk, and as their discomfort with what Jesus told them grew, they became more and more hesitant in their steps, less community oriented and more concerned about their own place in the future.

As we see in Mark 10:35-44, certain of the disciples were overconfident in their own abilities, lacking the dependence required of kingdom living. They audaciously believed they could stand beside Jesus and drink from His cup. But James and John did not have a monopoly on worldly-mindedness. The other disciples were indignant that two of the twelve tried to steal a march on them with Jesus.

Because these twelve men were the genesis of the coming church, in studying this section, I began to have some inkling of understanding of my own actions. As much as I hate to say it, none of us are exempt. We are "in the world" even if we are called not to be "of it." I can't help it sometimes — as much as I try for it not

---

[43] "Son of David" and "Messiah" are synonymous. Hendriksen, IBID., 419.

The Call to Follow Jesus

to be so, there are moments (or longer) when my halo goes awry and it's all about me. And as much as I hate to point the finger, I suspect if you're honest with yourself, I'm not alone.

Historical Quote

"Without somehow destroying me in the process, how could God reveal Himself in a way that would leave me no room for doubt? If there were no room for doubt, there would be no room for me."   - Frederick Buechner

Getting to the Heart of the Matter

Today's Reading: Mark 10:32-52
Parallel Passages: Matt. 20:27-34, Luke 18:31-43

Foretellings (Mark 10:32-45)

Read Mark 10:32-45.

1. **Make a list of those who were present with Jesus on the road to Jerusalem.**

2. **Mark 10:33-34 catalogs the third time that Jesus told the disciples what was going to happen to Him. (Mark 8:31, Mark 9:31) What things did He tell them?**

> Jesus did not remonstrate with them for wanting to be great, but He did revolutionize the standards by which greatness may be achieved. The path to greatness must lead to life in the kingdom or it cannot be great.

3. **Do you think Jesus had a need to talk about it for Himself, prepare His disciples for what was coming or a little of both?**

4. **How did the disciples respond to what Jesus told them?**

5. **In Mark 10:35-40, what did James and John tell Jesus they wanted Him to do for them?**

6. **What two things did Jesus tell them they must experience to meet the request?**

7. Do you think their request signified their understanding of kingdom living? Does the request in any way further kingdom living?

8. What do you learn about prayer from this discussion?

9. John Calvin says of James and John's request: "This narrative contains a bright mirror of human vanity, for it shows that proper and holy zeal is often accompanied by ambition…They who are not satisfied with Himself alone, but seek this or the other thing apart from Him and His promises, wander egregiously from the right path." How did the remaining disciples respond to James and John's request? (Mark 10:41)

> "For even the Son of Man did not come to be served, but to serve, and to give his life as a ransom for many"(Mark 10:45).

10. In Mark 10:42-45 Jesus taught the disciples about greatness in the kingdom by once again inverting it from the world's definition. How did He define greatness in this section?

11. How can your life better conform to Jesus' view of greatness?

12. Mark 10:45 is the key to the entire book of Mark. It is why Jesus came; it is why He began His ministry, calling and mentoring disciples, healing the sick and teaching the multitudes about kingdom living. What does this verse say is His purpose?

The phrase "ransom for many" in Greek is *anti-lutron*. *Lutron* means, "the price for redeeming, the ransom paid for slaves." *Anti* means *instead of*. The importance of the phrase must be understood. He put Himself in the place of the slaves (us) and paid the ransom for their freedom. Nothing less than His blood was the price paid.

Blind Bartimaeus: Sight Restored (Mark 10:46-52)

Scripture records that Bartimaeus' sight was restored and he followed Jesus. As Jesus continued toward Jerusalem, we hear no more of Bartimaeus but he "began following Jesus on the road" (Mark 10:52). There is something so uncomplicated and comforting about that statement. Here is Bartimaeus, the first one to publically declare Jesus' Messiahship; he might have been the instigator of the shouts and hosannas that filled the air as Jesus arrived in Jerusalem. He came to

Jesus knowing he was dependent, needy and aware of his incompetency to do anything for himself apart from Jesus' assistance. This was so unlike the disciples. We can't say for certain, but perhaps he was along for the duration of the journey to show the disciples what uncomplicated, simple, childlike faith in action looked like.

13. **In Mark 10:46 who was with Jesus as He entered Jericho?**

14. **What did Bartimaeus say to Jesus in Mark 10:47-48?**

15. **Do you feel the urgency in Bartimaeus' voice as he called out even louder amidst the crowd? Can you recall a moment of anxiety in your own life where you desperately needed to get someone's attention for some purpose of yours? Can you describe the feelings that urgency generated in your life?**

16. **What attitudes and characteristics do you see in Bartimaeus' life from the way he approached Jesus? (Mark 10:48-51)**

17. **What did Bartimaeus see that the disciples did not?**

18. **What road was Jesus on? As Bartimaeus followed on the same road, what might it have meant for his own future?**

19. **Review this chapter and jot down one or two concepts or principles that you think would help you as you live your life as a member of the kingdom.**

When Jesus asked Bartimaeus, "What do you want Me to do for you?" Bartimaeus the beggar could have asked for money, thinking sight was too much to ask for. It was a measure of his faith that he asked big. We can learn from what he asked for in our own lives. Do we ask for what is amazing, difficult, or impossible and expect God to act or do we ask for the mundane, the uncomplicated, the unnecessary? How big is your God?

Family Matters

This week I suggest a movie really outside the box. Produced by a church, the movie is about a young teen who disobeys her parents and ends up in a gang-related contest with tragic results. I definitely DO NOT recommend this for children, (though we let our young high school son watch it). If you are interested in an idea of what gehenna or hell will be like, this movie gives a frightening, realistic description. The name of the movie is *M10.28: The Movie*. It is available on Netflix and in some Christian bookstores.

Looking Forward

Next week we look into developing a kingdom mentality.

Chapter 7
Developing a Kingdom Mentality (Mark 11-12)

Day 1
One Day in a Million (Mark 11:1-14)

Background Information

There is a lot going on in today's lesson. More than what we traditionally call Palm Sunday, more than the triumphal entry of Jesus into Jerusalem on a donkey and more than waving palm branches, as if these things weren't enough!

The beginning of the Passion Week was a stealth day in history. It was a week in which monumental events in God's unfolding plan of redemption took place. There are prophetic statements in the Scriptures made hundreds of years before the actual day that predict *down to the very day* when the Messiah would enter Jerusalem coming on a donkey as the Servant King.

In those days people usually arrived in Jerusalem for the Passover on foot. Anyone who entered the city riding on anything was cause for comment. Also, how they came mattered. Clues were given to government officials as to the nature of the visit by the manner in which kings arrived. Conquering kings arrived in cities on white war horses; kings arriving on donkeys were known to come as "pursuing peace."

The Jews expected their Messiah to come to Jerusalem as a conquering king on a white war horse to set up the kingdom. No one was looking for Messiah on a donkey. And it is no wonder. The Scriptures predict two seemingly contradictory pictures of Messiah. One portrays Him from the lineage of David, coming to destroy the enemies of Israel and set up His kingdom; the other pictures Messiah as one who was gentle and humble, One who would suffer and die for the sins of His people. Some teachers even thought there would be *two* Messiahs. What few understood was that both pictures were true of One Messiah who would come twice.

Passion Week began with Jesus' arrival in Jerusalem on a donkey as prophesied. It proceeded to His arrest, trial, conviction, death and burial in a borrowed tomb ending with His glorious Resurrection. Unfortunately we do not get a strictly chronological following of events in Mark's gospel, but in true Mark style we get detail and a flavor of what was unfolding sufficient to understand how this important week was *the* week in history that changes everything!

In Mark 11 there is a rustling in the heavenly places as angels stand straighter and look more diligently into the doings of men; long foretold prophecies come to fruition on this day and those in the know are on the edge of their seats waiting for the next step in a plan that God has been revealing piece by piece in the pages of the Old Testament since its beginning in Genesis 3:15. It was this first day of Passion Week that Jesus publically announced His Messiahship through the manner of His arrival. It was the day historically believed to be the Sunday before Easter (Resurrection day).

The rest of Mark's gospel takes place in and around Jerusalem. With Jesus' entry the first day, He subsequently spent the evenings in nearby Bethany, returning the next day and the next, coming as a king would, checking out His new property (Mark 11:11). In typical Jesus style, He used a fig tree as a parable to teach His disciples the principles of fruit bearing, judgment and the power of prayer.

Disciples' Perspective

The disciples coming into Jerusalem with Jesus were unsure of what was actually happening, though they obeyed His commands. Peter who had stood stoutly before Jesus proclaiming Him as Messiah would soon deny all knowledge of Him. The stalwart brothers, James and John, who had so forcefully told Jesus that they could drink from His cup would soon be nowhere to be found. In the midst of a changeling crowd, Jesus stood alone to face the wrath of the underworld, the turning away of His Father and the force of the world's sins before and ever after His coming death.

Historical Quote

Charles deFocauld (1858-1916) was a French explorer known as "the hermit of the Sahara" He said, "Faith strips the mask from the world and reveals God in everything."

Getting to the Heart of the Matter

Today's Reading: Mark 11:1-14
Parallel Passages: Matt. 21:1-11, Luke 19:28-44, John 12:12-19

The reading today is the embodiment of fulfilled prophecy. To study the passage without understanding this would be a shallow endeavor. Jesus IS the Messiah. He IS the Savior. He IS the One of whom the prophets spoke and the fulfillment of the *first gospel* of Genesis 3:15.

As we look at today's passage I think the most powerful way to understand the depths of Scripture and Who Jesus is, would be to look at several Old Testament passages that prophecy His coming, His purpose, His death. We are committed to going through Mark verse by verse, but without background to illuminate the path, we would miss the unbelievable unfolding of the future and how it connects with everyday people living everyday lives.

In this section's *Background Information,* we explained the two pictures of Messiah depicted in the Old Testament. Both are descriptions of Jesus. His first arrival was as a humble, gentle, servant who was to suffer and die for the sins of His people. His second coming, still to come, will be as the conquering king (Rev. 9:11).[44]

1. **Review the following verses and state how the coming Messiah could be recognized:**

   (a) Isaiah 9:6-7

   (b) Isaiah 28:16-18

   (c) Isaiah 35:4-6

   (d) Isaiah 40:11

   (e) Isaiah 42:1-4

   (f) Isaiah 61:1-4 (Luke 4:18)

Jesus Enters Jerusalem on a Donkey (Mark 11:1-6)
Read Mark 11:1-6.

2. **From reading the *Background Information* above, how is Jesus' entrance different from how most people enter Jerusalem? Is there a message in His coming in this way?**

---

[44] Sir Robert Anderson, *The Coming Prince,* (Grand Rapids:Kregel, n.d.)

3. Read Num. 19:2; Deut. 21:3; 1 Sam. 6:7-8. What do these verses say about an animal who was to be used for a sacred purpose?

4. What sacred purpose can be seen in the Mark verses?

An animal devoted to a sacrificial purpose must be one that has not been put to work or ordinary use. When considered in terms of Jesus who was to be the Sacrificial Lamb, even the details have significance.

5. **Read Genesis 49:10-11. Is there any significance to the fact that the donkey/colt was tied? (Mark 11:2,4)**

Hosanna (Mark 11:7-10)

6. **In Mark 11:9-10, what words were the people shouting as Jesus passed them?**

The word *Hosanna* is a prayer that involves a saving action by God and literally means, "Save us."

7. **Review Psalm 118:22-29 and compare them with the words in Mark 11. Do you note any similarities?**

8. **Read Zechariah 9:9-10. What kind of king does Zechariah declare was coming in these verses? Are there any similarities to the verses in Mark?**

9. **How did the people view Jesus on the day described in Mark 11:1-10?**

Entering the Temple (Mark 11:11)

Some said that Jesus' entrance into the outer court of the temple was the "calm before the storm." Others have said that as the new King He was just looking over His property to see how it was being used.

10. **What did Jesus do in Mark 11:11?**

Cursing the Fig Tree (Mark 11:12-14)

Jesus used the fig tree as a parable (earthly story with a heavenly meaning). Most scholars believe that the fig tree represented Israel – all leaves, no fruit. Others have said that the fig tree is a picture of the terrible judgment that awaited Jerusalem (when it was later destroyed in AD 70).

The Call to Follow Jesus

11. **Look up the following verses and write down your thoughts on what Jesus' actions in this passage might refer to:**

(a) **Hos. 2:12 (in a passage describing the condemnation of unfaithful Israel)**

(b) **Isa. 34:4 (in a passage concerning God's wrath against nations)**

(c) **Jer. 8:13 (in a section of Scripture describing Judah's sin and treachery)**

The significance of the Triumphal Entry into Jerusalem on Palm Sunday cannot be understated. Parallel passages in the gospels expose that the religious leaders were distraught because they understood the method of Jesus' coming (Luke 20:37-40). In addition to the many prophecies concerning this particular passage which you examined today, there is one other, perhaps *the* single most important prophecy concerning Messiah's coming.

In Dan. 9:24-25 and Neh. 2:1 we are givens a series of dates telling the arrival of "Messiah the Prince" to "…finish the transgression, to make an end of sin, to make atonement for iniquity to bring in everlasting righteousness…" (Daniel 9:24 NASB).

Using the dates given (and others in Scripture), scholars have mapped out the "70 weeks of Daniel" discussed in Daniel 9 and determined that the length of the period intervening between the issuing of the decree to rebuild Jerusalem and the public advent of "Messiah the Prince" would be exactly 173,880 days. They also determined from examining the Jewish calendars and the Julian calendar that the final day fell on the *exact date* that Jesus publically rode into Jerusalem on a donkey (Mark 11:1-10).[45] This is amazing! Simply put, unless some other Messiah rode into Jerusalem on a donkey on the same day Jesus did, Jesus is positively and definitely who He claims to be!

The crowds welcomed Jesus enthusiastically, even if they failed to understand the significance of the day. They laid out their branches and their clothing and waved palm leaves and gave praise to God asking Him to "save us" (Hosanna). But how fickle we humans are for it was not a week later that the same crowd was calling

---

[45] *The Coming Prince*, IBID., Chapter 10

for Jesus' crucifixion. The disciples had dispersed in fear of being likewise taken up, and Jesus was alone.

I see myself in that crowd, much as I wish I didn't. I want to be faithful and true and worthy of His stand on my behalf but I fail so often. Thank God you and I don't get what we deserve. Instead we get what He came for – forgiveness, eternal life and a Friend Whose Presence is always with us.

Day 2
"Something is Rotten in the State of Denmark" (Mark 11:15-33)

Background Information

Today's study title comes from an oft recognized Shakespeare quote from *Hamlet*, Act 1, Scene IV though the phrase was not spoken by Prince Hamlet himself as is often believed, but by a minor player, Marcellus. After observing what was happening at court, Marcellus made the comment, "Something is rotten in the state of Denmark," to refer to the fact that all is not well at the top. We use the phrase today to also signify that, "something fishy is going on" in political and other arenas where problems often start at the top and work their way down to impact the rest of the masses.

In this section Jesus confronted the rottenness in and around Jerusalem. When it was time for Passover, the city began to fill with devout Jews and converts. As people came into the city, businesses set up stalls where people could buy animals and others items needed for the ceremonial sacrifices which took place during Passover. Stalls were also set up where foreigners who needed to exchange their currency could do so, for a fee of course. It became big business and somewhere along the line, the outer court of the Jewish temple (called the "Court of the Gentiles") was also taken over for the purpose of buying, selling and exchanging currency. This precluded non-Jews who wanted to convert to Judaism from worshiping and seeking God since that was the only part of the temple they could enter.

Jesus and His disciples passed by the fig tree which they had seen the day before to find it completely withered, with no fruit, not unlike the leaders in the temple Jesus had just cast out. He used the tree as a parable to teach the disciples about the fruit of their own lives.

Finally, as Jesus entered the temple again, He was confronted by a pack of Jewish leaders outraged at Jesus' audacity in not only kicking out the entrepreneurs, but in using the very action to teach His listeners more truth.

Disciples' Perspective

There is a new energy building in Jesus as He neared the Cross. His detractors were likewise energetic in their frenzy to have Him gone. Not only was Jesus becoming more forceful in His confrontations, He was more direct in His conversations with His disciples as He sought to establish their faith and develop kingdom mentality into their being. By comparing their own potential for fruit against that of the withered fig tree they were learning lessons concerning those who called themselves leaders of the true faith.

Historical Quote

"The house of my soul is too small. Enlarge it so you can enter in, Lord."

-St. Augustine

Getting to the Heart of the Matter

Today's Reading: Mark 11:15-33,
Parallel Passages: Matt. 21:12-27, Luke 19:45-48, Luke 20:1-8

Cleansing the Temple (Mark 11:15-19)

Read Mark 11:15-19.

> Even in the Old Testament God called His temple a "house of prayer for all nations." Isa. 56:7. Does this have any meaning for us today?

1. **What did Jesus do in Mark 11:15-16?**

2. **Who do you think were Jesus' hearers in Mark 11:17?**

3. **What was the message Jesus gave to His hearers?**

4. **Where is God's temple today? (Clue: 1 Cor. 6:19)**

5. **How did the chief priests and scribes respond to Jesus' message?**

6. **What impact did the buyers and sellers in the temple have on non-Jewish converts?**

7. **Do you think Jesus' actions had any impact on anyone else other than those He directly spoke to in this section?**

8. **Review Jer. 7:1-11. Answer the following questions:**

   (a) Make a list of the "If you…" phrases God tells Judah (11:1-6).

   (b) What will God do IF Judah obeys (11:7)?

   (c) What are the people of Judah trusting in (11:8)?

   (d) What deceptions were the people involved in (11:9-11)?

9. **Is there a message for us today in the Jeremiah passage?**

Lesson of the Fig Tree (Mark 11:20-26)

The lesson of the fig tree is all about "fruit bearing." Jesus cursed it because it contained no fruit. Using the tree as a parable of what they had just seen in the temple, the Jewish leaders, who represented the "roots of the fruit trees," were entrusted with the job of being God's fruit bearers. They were failing miserably. Instead of dispensing faith, they piled more fruitless tasks and laws on a people already over-burdened. Just as a fruit tree is planted in order to bear fruit, so are our lives given in order that we bear His fruit. Jesus wanted to impress this lesson strongly upon His disciples: that faith is the secret of fruitfulness in their lives.

10. **Read Mark 11:20. How had the fig tree withered? Do you see any significance in this?**

11. **Who called the withered fig tree to Jesus' attention (Mark 11:21)?**

12. **How did Jesus answer Peter (Mark 11:22)? What did His answer to Peter have to do with the fig tree?**

13. **What was the main topic of Mark 11:23-24? What specific things did Jesus tell His disciples about this topic?**

In the eastern culture, the culture in which the Bible was written, certain words have symbolic meaning. For instance, the word *mountain* in middle-eastern culture is often a symbolic word for nations, kingdoms or empires. (Isa. 2:2-3) This brings about an interesting point about prayer, doesn't it? But, as we have already learned, Scripture does not always have only one meaning – it is layered and we can learn different concepts from each verse. So while there are implications in how we pray to move mountains in the eastern thought process, there is also implication for our personal prayer life as it relates to our world.

14. **What do you think Jesus meant when He said faith can move mountains? Is there a mountainous task in your life that God has given to you?**

15. **How about prayer to move the mountain of our own nation toward God?**

Rabbis in Jesus' time were sometimes called "mountain removers" because they taught their disciples how to remove the mountain of ignorance and confusion from men's minds.[46]

In a small corner of my Bible I have written the words: "Forgiveness is a willingness to bear the wrong done against me so someone who has wronged me can go free. It means to bear the pain of someone else's wrong." Probably taken from a sermon or program I was listening to, I am sorry that I cannot give credit to who said it because they are powerful words.

16. **We have learned in prior lessons that unbelief impacts the power of our prayers. In Mark 11:25-26 there is another obstacle that blocks the power of prayer. What is it?**

17. **Write your own definition of forgiveness here.**

18. **Is there something someone has done to you that you are harboring in your heart which needs to be exposed and forgiven? Write it here.**

---

[46] Ogilvie, IBID., 222.

Chapter 7. Developing a Kingdom Mentality (Mark 11-12)

19. What are the "lessons of the fig tree" that you see Jesus giving to His disciples in these verses? What does faith have to do with the lessons you see?

The Temple Confrontation (Mark 11:27-33)
Read Mark 11:27-33.

20. Who confronted Jesus in Mark 11:27-28? For what purpose?

21. What *things* do you think they are referring to in Mark 11:28?

22. How did Jesus answer them?

23. What was their answer and reasoning?

24. What can you learn about this encounter for your own witness today?

I find it interesting that the example of the fig tree is couched between two confrontations in the temple. This tells me that there is a connection. The fig tree and the temple are just different pictures of the same truth that Jesus is teaching His disciples. Both are fruitless. The tree's fruitlessness is masked by leaves, while in the Temple, the outward busyness of the activities obscured the fact that no worship was actually taking place there. But I can't in good conscience cast the first stone. Sometimes the fruit in my life is pretty obscure and insignificant too.

It is amazing, though, how single-focused Jesus is. He knew He was within days of the Cross and He was determined to get there, but along the way, He was also determined to pour into His disciples every lesson He could. Do you see the kingdom message today? We have seen Jesus pour it in over and over and over again.

In the Parable of the Sower (God being the sower), He chooses to *work through us;* in today's lesson of the fig tree, He pours faith into us so we can be fruit bearers and nourishers so *He can work through us.*

I can never get over why He would choose someone as insignificant as me to entrust to help with the growth of others' faith. But thankfully, it is Him working through me (and you) — not something we generate on our own. It is kingdom living at its best, isn't it? We get the joy and blessing of serving and seeing fruit from our labors and He does the work of ripening the fruit.

Day 3
Foretelling of a Future Murder (Mark 12:1-12)

Background Information

In first century Galilee many landowners were absentee owners who leased the land to tenant farmers to farm their land in exchange for a portion of the harvest. This created an inevitable tension as the farmers resented the rich owners and believed that because the farmers did the work, they should receive all of the benefits.

Lane in his commentary informs us that today's parable, "...belongs to the general category of judgment parables; it is a dramatic presentation of a life situation which invites a judgment from the hearers."[47] Jesus used the familiar parable to expose the Pharisees and their attempts on His own life. He also used a familiar passage from Isaiah 5 so there could be no misunderstanding regarding who the parable was pointing toward.

There was a lot of history contained in this story and educated hearers could not mistake its meaning. In the story, Jesus also told the Jewish leaders what they were planning every step of the way. He charged them with murder before the deed was even done. This parable also predicted the tragic devastation of Jerusalem and destruction of the temple AD 70, just a few years in the future.

But the story is so much more than a history lesson. It also showed the Father's longsuffering and patience in His attempts throughout Jewish history to bring the vine-growers/tenant farmers (or Jewish leaders) back to the Father's love by sending prophets over and over again with His message of repentance and forgiveness. When the prophets continually failed to reach Israel, just as in this story, He sent His beloved Son to try again to express His love for His people.

Jesus' reference to Psalm 118:22-23 in the passage was a clear message to His hearers that He was the son referenced in the parable and contrasted His despised status by the Jewish leaders with His glorious, exalted position which God intended for Him at the appointed time. There could be no escaping the meaning of this story to both the disciples and the Jewish leaders.

---

[47] Lane, IBID., 416.

Disciples' Perspective

The disciples were entirely silent as Jesus told this parable to the Jewish leaders. They were, however listening and learning. After Pentecost, Peter and the others came to understand Jesus' meaning in this and so many other things He told them (See for example, Acts 4:11, 1 Pet. 2:7). And we are like them as we grow in our faith too. We may not understand things the first time around, but as we stay the course and remain faithful to seeking Him, we grow and learn. What was once foggy and unclear often comes back to our remembrance as fresh, new lessons.

Historical Quote

"It was pride that caused the fall of Lucifer and Adam. If you should ask me what are the ways of God, I would tell you that the first is humility, the second is humility and the third is still humility. Not that there are no other precepts to give but humility, but if humility does not precede all that we do, our efforts are fruitless."
                                                                   -St. Augustine

Getting to the Heart of the Matter

Today's Reading: Mark 12:1-12
Parallel Passages: Matt. 23:33-46, Luke 20:9-19

1. **Review the definition of a parable and write it here (See Chapter 3, Day 1 for help).**

2. **Who was the story addressed to (Mark 11:18)?**

3. **Who was present in the story?**

4. **Read Isa. 5:1-7 and compare that section of Scripture with this section. What parallels do you see in the two passages?**

5. **Read Amos 3:7, Zech. 1:6. What designation is given to the prophets sent by God to warn the Jews? What part do they play in this parable?**

6. **If a parable is defined as *an earthly story with a heavenly meaning*, what/who do you think the following refer to?**

   (a) The landowner

(b) The tenants

(c) The servants

(d) The landowner's son

It is quite possible that the arrival of the son in the story might have led the tenants to believe the father had died and that by killing the son, they might be able to claim the inheritance. There were some laws in Jewish society which allowed "ownerless land" to be claimed by anyone.

7. **Do you think it was unrealistic of the tenants to assume the father was dead and by killing the son, they might claim the inheritance? Why?**

8. **What was the consequence of rejection of the son in the story (Mark 2:9)?**

9. **How about the spiritual meaning of rejecting the son?**

10. **What does it teach us for our own spiritual life?**

11. **Who do you think the *others* were, as referred to in Mark 12:9?**

Read Psalm 118:22-23[48]. The passage refers to one of the building blocks for Solomon's temple which was rejected during its construction. It later proved to be the key stone in Solomon's porch. It is also a prophetical verse about the coming of Messiah.

12. **How does Ps. 118:22-23 tie in to Mark 12:10-11?**

---

[48] Just for your information, Psalm 118:8 is the exact middle verse of the Bible. It is a verse worth memorizing.

13. **Why didn't the Jewish leaders seize Jesus once the meaning of the story became clear to them (Mark 12:12)?**

This story ended the third day of Passover week. The Cross was now only a few days away, yet we see no evidence of anxiety or nervousness on Jesus' part, but more of a resolute spirit that will not waver. Watch for clues in the remaining chapters of how Jesus handles what He knows is coming. What can you learn from Him about your own anxiety?

Day 4
Sadducees, Pharisees, Scribes, Oh My! (Mark 12:13-37)

Background Information

In today's lesson we will probe at least one worldview[49] in existence in Jesus' day. If you look carefully, you will see remnants of those beliefs present in some worldviews people adopt today.

The amazing thing about Scripture is that there is order, meaning and truth behind every story, encounter and parable. Even the sequence of the questions brought to Jesus by the various Jewish factions have meaning. According to D. Daube[50], there are four types of questions asked of Jesus in today's lesson which were typical of the type of question recognized by Rabbis as being asked during Passover:

- The *wisdom* question (Mark 12:13-17), which usually addressed a point of Jewish law
- Questions of *mockery*, which centered on the question of the resurrection – a subject the Sadducees did not believe in, you recall (Mark 12:18-27)
- Questions of *conduct*, which generally referred to the relationship between God and men (Mark 12:28-34)
- Questions of *Biblical exegesis*, usually addressing apparent conflicts or contradictions in the Scripture (Mark 12:35-37)

Disciples' Perspective

Opposition dogged Jesus and afterwards, his disciples, as they lived out their call. In this lesson the disciples were watching the continued battering of Jesus by the different factions who hated Him.

---

[49] A 'worldview' is how we look at the world. Everyone has one. kingdom living implies members of the kingdom look at life and the world from God's perspective.

[50] Quoted at Lane, IBID., 421.

It was another layer of learning as they watched how Jesus answered trick questions and side-stepped clever traps. Note the difference between how Jesus handled the hardened Pharisees who were in no way seeking truth, and how He addressed, with a sense of compassion, the young scribe who approached Him. Jesus discerned that the rich young ruler might be a truth-seeker. The disciples and we too, must learn to discern between those who are sincerely seeking and those who are not.

Historical Quote

Henri Nouwen, in *The Road to Daybreak* wrote about the rich young ruler. He says that Jesus loved him and probably wanted to call him as a disciple. "But the young man's life was too complex; he had too many things to worry about; too many affairs to take care of; too many people to relate to. He couldn't let go of his concerns, and thus, disappointed and downcast, he left Jesus…"

Getting to the Heart of the Matter

Today's Reading: Mark 12:13-44
Parallel Passages: Matt. 22:15-22

The Pharisees and Herodians (Mark 12:13-17)

In this section, Jesus was bombarded with cleverly portrayed word-traps by various opponents hoping to trip Him into a careless answer, thus getting somebody mad at Him. Taxes were a big deal in Jesus' day just as they are today. Though Julius Caesar reduced taxes during his reign, the Herod family came along and picked up the slack by implementing taxes on fishing, port dues and tolls. This was in addition to religious dues ranging from 10 to 20 percent of the Jews' income before other taxes were paid. The Jews generally paid between 30 and 40 percent of their income on taxes and religious dues. The Pharisees in particular hated taxes so it is interesting to note their teaming up with the Herodians to confront Jesus.

Keep in mind as you read this section, that the only coin accepted in the Roman territory was the Roman denarius which portrayed the emperor as a god. The usage of the coinage implicitly acknowledged Caesar's authority and an obligation to pay the taxes demanded. Jesus' answer to the Pharisees' questions recognized that there are obligations of the state which do not infringe upon God's rights. (This was later discussed by Paul, Rom. 13:1-7 and Peter in 1 Pet. 2:13-17.)

On the other hand, Jesus' masterful answer also protected God's rights. By sharply distinguishing between the two, He tacitly protested against the idolatrous claims put forth on the coins. Divine honors belong to God alone. Jesus' whole life and teaching exhibited that duties to God and the state are not completely separate. They are united but ruled by the higher principles of accomplishing in all things the will of God in the lives of men, thus once again highlighting kingdom living.

1. **Who was present in Mark 12:13-17?**

The question asked here was designed as a master-trap. If Jesus answered in the affirmative, He would be discredited among the people for whom the tax was a terrible burden. If He answered in the negative, He would invite Roman reprisal and investigation as a zealot.

2. **What was the question that the Jewish leaders asked Jesus?**

3. **How did Jesus answer the question?**

Jesus' answer to the Pharisees and Herodians was a master answer! In a word, Jesus denounced the self-righteousness of the Pharisees and the self-indulgence of the Herodians.

4. **Do you see how He did it? If so, explain your anwer.**

5. **The phrase, "Render to Caesar what belongs to Caesar" actually pleased the Pharisees. What do you think it means and why would it please the Pharisees?**

6. **The phrase, "Render to God the things that are God's" actually has to do with kingdom living. What was Jesus trying to tell His hearers by this statement?**

The Sadducees Question Jesus (Mark 13:18-27)

Josephus tells us that the Sadducees represented the urban, wealthy sophisticated class centered in Jerusalem. They were a small group of educated and prominent men. The group disappeared from the historical scene after the devastation of Jerusalem in AD 70 and, according to some scholars, none of their documents

> **Kingdom living is not achieved by political posturing, improving welfare conditions or entitlement programs. These issues resolve when kingdom living is occurring. Jesus' kingdom is all about the inner life and the state of men's hearts. What belongs to God must never be demanded of Caesar or any other living person. Our hearts, should we choose to give them, belong solely to God.**

have survived. From today's perspective, their worldview was a *closed worldview*. In other words, they were the naturalists who didn't believe in miracles, angels, signs or wonders, like many scientists today.

7. **Write down what else you remember about the Sadducees. If you can't recall, refer to the *Background Information* of Chapter 2, Day 1.**

8. **Summarize the question they posed to Jesus (Mark 12:19-23).**

Actually, in *this life* the Sadducees were correct in their assessment of the law. The principles they mention about whose wife the woman will be in the resurrection (which they didn't believe in) is described in the kinsman redeemer story found in *The Book of Ruth*. The question was: is it the same in the next life and, even more elementary, *is* there a next life?

> **The Sadducees missed the point that if men still live after death, God could certainly make that life different from the life in this world. This would make their question meaningless.**

9. **What two things did Jesus accuse them of in Mark 12:24?**

10. **What was His answer to the question, and what belief of theirs did He wipe out by His answer (Mark 12:25)?**

11. **In Mark 12:26 Jesus focused on their ignorance of Scripture by quoting from their own Old Testament books (the Torah or first five books of the Old Testament).**

    (a) **By quoting from Exodus 3:1-17, what did He say about the burning bush and what God said to Moses?**

    (b) **What does this imply about whether Moses, Abraham, Isaac and Jacob were alive or dead at the time of this encounter?**

12. **In Mark 12:27 Jesus pinpointed their lack of belief in God's power. What did He say to them about God's power?**

13. Do you know people who are locked up in a small box with a closed worldview like the Sadducees? Is there anything in how Jesus speaks to the Sadducees that could help you as you relate to them?

The Scribe (Mark 12:28-34)

During Jesus' day, there were approximately 613 laws. Of those, 365 were negative and 248 were positive. Rabbis in those days either split the law into infinitely small sections or tried to synthesize and summarize it for their students. Scribes generally believed that all laws had equal authority which made the following discourse another trap for Jesus.

14. **What question did the scribe ask Jesus?**

Read Deuteronomy 6:4-5. This command is called the *Shema* which means "He is One." It is considered among most Jews as the most important command in the entire Law. Devoted Jews still quote it at least twice a day. It also has major implications for kingdom living as Jesus here and elsewhere confirmed its major importance.

15. **In Mark 12:29-30, what does God require of us?**

16. **Which of the things God requires do you find hardest to turn over to His keeping?**

17. **By combining a second command with the *Shema*, Jesus showed the outcome of actually trying to live out the *Shema*. What did Mark 12:31 add to the requirement of loving God?**

18. **Who is your neighbor? Are there some people in your world that you are having trouble loving? Name them here. Commit to pray for them and ask God to free you so He can love them through you. What would that look like?**

19. **Read Mark 12:33-34. From Jesus' answer, what do you think was the state of the scribe's heart?**

I've always been a bit bummed out by Jesus' affirmation that, "there will be no marriage in heaven." I like my husband and don't want to think of life here or there without him. On the other hand, some of you might be glad to let go of an unhappy relationship in the after-life. There is hope for us all!

Various authors I have come across in my reading for this session seem to indicate that "no marriage" does not mean there will be no intimacy or pleasure in heaven. But it probably does mean some type of shift – one that we will not regret losing. The great purpose of our eternity will be about worship, serving, using our gifts, experiencing joy, loving God and loving others with a pure, untainted love. As Rick Warren said in the first sentence of *The Purpose Driven Life*, "It's not about you." But it is about being in close community with the One and Only. And that is something to look forward to!

Day 5
Which Messiah is He? (Mark 12:35-44)

Background Information

I know of a family whose aunt was widowed and lived alone. She was a school teacher all her life but was frugal, invested well and bought stock in companies that thrived. She was also committed to her local church and tithed regularly. Unfortunately, she was not as astute in choosing a church as she was in choosing stock. When the pastor discovered how well off she was, he moved his whole family into her home, promising to "take care" of her until her death. Her family was unable to convince her to exercise discretion and wisdom in this instance and she refused to hear anything against the pastor or his family. She died in poverty.

This is not a story I really wanted to share with you but I also feel compelled to tell things like they are. While most pastors have a genuine call on their lives and are faithful to the core, history reports that there have also been charlatans taking advantage of those who need the most protection.

This is a subject that Jesus likewise took up in today's study. Rabbis and scribes were not paid salaries (it was forbidden). They relied on benefactors and patrons for gifts and subsidies. Not surprisingly, although highly respected, many of them belonged to the poorer classes. Some, seeking to raise their financial level by using their high standing, took advantage of women and widows. They sometimes encroached on their hospitality (not unlike the story above). They robbed the poor and grieving under guises of personal piety which doubled the guilt. Still, people stood when a scribe walked by. They were highly valued as guests at parties. They were given seating preference over everyone else, including the aged and their own parents. It was considered an act of personal holiness to relieve a scribe of concern for his living expenses.

Unfortunately, like us, they were in danger of losing perspective in the One they were really serving and often lost focus in the day-to-day need for existence.

Jesus also further clarified His standing as not only the suffering Messiah but also as the reigning Messiah that David acknowledged in Psalm 110:1. The prophetic promise to David served as the starting point to proclaiming Jesus as Savior. His resurrection and exaltation mark the fulfillment of the promise.

Disciples' Perspective

One of the skills necessary to being a disciple is the ability to see (not necessarily visually) and observe. It is, I think, a learned skill, one that can be taught as we absorb the Scriptures and observe the world around us. God calls us to integrate and bring to our world what He teaches us through our reading of the Word, what we learn through our trials and suffering, and what we see happening around us. We don't have the physical Jesus to hang on to, and very soon the disciples will be in our boat. Their very lives were being turned inside out by following in the Master's footsteps but He kept them ever on His radar.

You also can be sure that you are never out of His sight. I once had a bumper sticker on my car that said, "Wherever you are, God is." It was comforting to me, but to others it was an irritating reminder that His eyes are always on us. Which camp are you in today? Are you involved in things that you hope no one sees? If so, I have to disappoint you – He is with you.

Historical Quote

"Life is a journey toward a land we have not yet seen along a path we sometimes cannot find. It is a journey of the soul toward its destiny and its home."
-Larry Crabb

Getting to the Heart of the Matter

Today's Reading: Mark 12:35-44
Parallel Passages: Matt. 22:21-46, Luke 20:41-47, Luke 21:1-4

Read Mark 12:35-37 and Psalm 110:1. Jesus invoked thoughtful pondering among His listeners in this section today by asking an exegetical question (refer to Chapter 7, Day 4 for a reminder). If David referred to Messiah as his Lord, he understood that the One who received the promise is far greater than he is and is not really his son.

1. **Let's try to answer Jesus' own question: What did the scribes mean when they said the Messiah was the son of David? Write your thoughts about this question.**

David himself distinguished between his own earthly sovereignty as king and the total sovereignty assigned to the Messiah. The Messiah is not only the son of David, but is also the Lord. His role was to establish the eternal kingdom. It always comes back to that, doesn't it? That Jesus the Messiah came not to establish an earthly kingdom but a heavenly one. "Repent for the kingdom of heaven is at hand," becomes clearer and clearer as we continue our study through Mark.

Jesus knew that this was His week – the Passion Week. He also knew His battle was not for that moment in time, but for all eternity. Read 2 Cor. 10:3-7.

2. **Describe Jesus' battle as it is fought through us.**

3. **What does this section say about the crowd listening to Jesus? Does this give you any clue as to their spiritual state?**

4. **Read Mark 12:38-40. How did Jesus describe the scribes?**

5. **Do you know people like this today? What type of person would fit this description?**

6. **In Mark 12:41-44, what is the contrast between how the scribes lived and how this widow lived?**

7. **What did Jesus have to say about the woman?**

8. **What lesson(s) were Jesus teaching His disciples from this situation?**

> Jesus' relationship with the scribes was not always strained, as seen in His earlier encounter with the scribe in Mark 12:28-34.

> How did Jesus know the amount of the widow's gift? Some scholars point to the thirteen trumpet shaped receptacles located in the "Court of the Women" in the Tabernacle where people left their gifts. While not stated in Mark, it is suggested that a gift's amount and purpose was audibly pronounced to the priest when placed in one of the receptacles.

9. **What was the value of the two small coins against the large givers? What heavenly things could be accomplished by the woman's gift, small as it was?**

10. **What can we learn about our own giving patterns from this story?**

11. **Review this chapter and jot down one or two concepts or principles that you think would help you as you live your life as a member of the kingdom.**

12. **What did she bring that was *more than* just a few coins?**

The disciples failed to appreciate the woman's total commitment to God, which is by far the greater gift. Just this morning I was singing (to myself) a song by Michael Smith, *Heart of Worship* and thinking about the words. God requires and desires so much more than just our shallow offerings. The nameless widow in today's lesson understood this. We can all learn something from her life.

Family Matters

This week I recommend you purchase a CD or this song from Michael W. Smith called *Heart of Worship*. The lyrics are incredible as are all of his songs.

> When the music fades
> All is stripped away
> And I simply come
> Longing just to bring
> Something that's of worth
> That will bless Your heart
> I'll bring You more than a song
> For a song in itself
> Is not what You have required
> You search much deeper within
> Through the way things appear
> You're looking into my heart
>
> Chorus: I'm coming back to the heart of worship
> And it's all about You,
> It's all about You, Jesus
> I'm sorry, Lord, for the thing I've made it

The Call to Follow Jesus

When it's all about You,
It's all about You, Jesus

King of endless worth
No one could express
How much You deserve
Though I'm weak and poor
All I have is Yours
Every single breath
I'll bring You more than a song
For a song in itself
Is not what You have required
You search much deeper within
Through the way things appear
You're looking into my heart

Chorus

I encourage you to meditate on these words, listen to the song and think about the widow in today's lesson.

Chapter 8
Deeper into the Call (Mark 13)

Day 1
Life Alert, Part One (Mark 13:1-23)

We are all fascinated by the future:

- *What will happen?*
- *What is coming?*
- *When will these things occur?*

These are questions we often hear even today. Mark introduced a new style of writing in Chapter 13, the *apocalyptic style,* where he spoke in terms of revelation and prophecy. This literary style is similar to Daniel and Revelation. It means the publication of something unknown up to the time the revelation is given. Its general purpose is to declare God's pre-determined will to the world and speaks to man regarding the future.

As Jesus spoke to His disciples on what was coming in the future, He gave them what I call "Life Alert" keys. Sixteen different times in this chapter, Jesus gave His disciples a command or an imperative of what to do in the midst of the turmoil that was coming – both near in time to them, and far in time for future disciples such as you and me. Jesus actually told His disciples not only what would happen, but more importantly, how they should respond.

Jesus is intensely practical in teaching us lessons in kingdom living. Life Alert keys are messages to help us be watchful and alert in the midst of tribulation, persecution and suffering (both private and corporate).

Background Information

As we proceed in today's study, more than ever I want to remind you of the lesson of the onion: that Scripture is often layered with more than one meaning for more than one epoch in time. From the beginning of the chapter, Jesus told His disciples that destruction was coming to the temple. The phrase in Mark 13:2 "not one stone will remain" is prophetical of the coming Jewish War (AD 66-70) when the temple was destroyed in AD 70 by General Titus (later emperor Titus) thus ending the Jewish rebellion.[51]

Mark's hearers probably were living through that very time or very near to it. It was actually a time of great fear for the people of the day. There were both natural and political disasters. One scholar noted that between this prophecy by Jesus and the destruction of Jerusalem there were earthquakes in Crete (AD 46 or 47), Rome (AD 51), Apamaia in Phrygia (AD 60), and Campania (AD 63). He notes also four famines during the reign of Claudius from AD 41-54. One of them was in Judea in AD 44 and is alluded to in Acts 11:28. Tacitus (*Annals* xvi. 10-13) described hurricanes and storms in Campania in AD 65. If that weren't enough, rebels were threatening the republic of Rome and Jerusalem was a huge target. The people could easily have thought the end of the world was near.

The Jewish War is well documented by Josephus and others. In AD November 66 Jewish forces won an early victory over Titus' 12th Roman legion, pushing them back for a time. However, astute people, perhaps with Jesus' very words (Mark 13:14-23) ringing in their ears, fled the city. Recognizing that no one ever won a military battle against Rome, people began leaving in droves. At first they freely left the city, fleeing to a nearby hillside called Pella (Perea) where they waited out the war.

People were allowed to leave the city without restraint until the spring of AD 68 when efforts were put in place to halt desertions. Josephus records that in the spring of 68, the rivers of the Jordan were swollen due to recent rainstorms, thus preventing fugitives from Gadarene from crossing over to seek refuge. Thus it was doubly difficult to flee during those last days.

The War ended in AD 70 with Titus overwhelming the city, slaughtering millions (according to Josephus) and destroying the city by setting fire to it.

There was so much gold in the temple, and the fire was so hot that much of it melted into the cracks of the stones. Romans carried the stones away to get at the gold, thus completing Jesus' prophecy of not one stone remaining. (Luke 19:41-44)[52] Josephus wrote, "No one visiting the city would believe it had ever been inhabited."

The same words could have prophetic meaning for us today as well, though most scholars seem to agree that the first part of Mark 13 (:5-23) spoke of the coming Jewish War and second part of Mark 13 (:24-37) speaks of Christ's second coming (which has not yet occurred).

---

[51] It is also reminiscent of when the first Temple was destroyed by Antiochus Epiphanes in BC 168.

[52] Dr. Arnold Fructenbaum, *In the Footsteps of the Messiah*, (Ariel Publications: 2003 Ariel Publications), 623.

I do not plan in this chapter to sort out what exactly Jesus meant and precisely when in time these things are to occur. We can however, start with the premise that they *will* occur if they have not already and we must be ready.

If you are interested in prophecy as a study (and who isn't in these times?), there are many excellent resources and study guides to help you.

Jesus used the disciples' questions as a starting point, a method of teaching. He used their questions as a backdrop to teach them about *how* to prepare for the future, not just *what and when* things will happen. As we continue to explore kingdom living in the midst of a twisted world, the sixteen Life Alert keys Jesus gave as tools will help us *prepare* for what surely is coming so that we will *be ready, alert and watchful.*

Disciples' Perspective

As discussed above, Jesus used the disciples' questions as a backdrop or an opportunity to talk of future things, not with the purpose of scaring them, but to empower them to remain faithful in the midst, and as a way to infuse strength into weary believers. He used the set stage of what will happen in the future to encourage His beloved to remain faithful to kingdom living and the call to obedience. What the disciples were just beginning to realize was that they had just received the call to cross-bearing and the evangelization of all nations. Even so, come quickly, Lord Jesus!

Historical Quote

"Preparation of last things is to concentrate on first things."
- Lloyd Ogilvie

> In Rabbinical teaching the phrase "nation against nation" is a Jewish idiom referring to a world war. According to historical information, the first world war was World War I.

Getting to the Heart of the Matter

Today's Reading: Mark 13:1-23
Parallel Passages: Matt. 24:1-28, Luke 21:5-24

Signs of the End – Olivet Discourse (Mark 13)

Read Mark 13:1-4.

1. **What audience is Mark writing to? (refer to Chapter One, Day One) What are they going through at the time of this writing (approximately 62-66 AD)?**

2. **Who is present in this scene (Mark 13:3)?**

"These things" in Mark 13:4 refer to destruction of the temple, but were not indicators of end times theology.

3. **What two questions did Jesus' disciples ask (Mark 13:4)?**

There are basically three signs given in this chapter. The first sign seen in Mark 13:5-8, told of the beginning of sorrows and started with confusion created by wars, earthquakes and famines. Jesus warned against misreading the significance of these events. They were "merely the beginning" of birth pangs.

Anyone who has ever had a child knows that the beginning of birth pangs speaks of more intense pain and suffering still to come and that pangs leading up to the birth become closer in time and more painful.

The second sign is seen in Mark 13:14, "when the abomination of desolation is standing where it should not be standing", it is time to flee. This is historically believed by scholars to be General Titus who entered the temple in AD 70 before destroying it and committing unimaginable sacrilege there. The High Priest at that time was heard to say that he wished he had died before seeing such an outrage occur in the beloved Temple.

The third sign, which scholars believe heralds in Jesus' Second Coming and returning as conquering king (Mark 13:25-37) is seen by upheavals in nature and unusual occurrences. These things are yet to come.

False Prophets Coming (Mark 13:5-8)
Read Mark 13:5-8.

4. **What two commands or imperatives (Life Alert keys) did Jesus give to the disciples in these verses?**

> **"Birth pangs" in Rabbinic literature is a technical term that signified a period of intense suffering that would take place prior to Messianic deliverance.**

5. **In the first imperative, Jesus warned the disciples against false prophets. How can we recognize them (:5-6)?**

6. **What form of spiritual deception do you think our society is most vulnerable to today?**

7. How can we test the claims of those doing miracles who claim to be Christ-followers?

We have all seen false prophets who rise up and take captive a host of people who follow them to their destruction. Jesus warned the disciples against their *deception*, how they manifest themselves. Many who are still yet to come will claim to be sent by Jesus or even to BE the Messiah, taking the title and authority which belongs to Jesus alone. The warning is to "see to it" so that we are not led astray.

8. **From what you have learned from this study so far, what things can you to do prepare and "see to it" that you are not one of those deluded?**

9. **What things did Jesus tell the disciples are the "beginning of birth pangs"? Have you seen any of these signs today?**

10. **What was the warning Jesus gave when these things are seen and experienced? (Mark 13:7)**

Persecution (Mark 13:9-13)

Persecution under Nero gave believers a taste of what Jesus was saying in these passages.

11. **What three imperatives or commands (Life Alert keys) did Jesus give to His hearers in these verses (Mark 13:9, 10, 13)?**

12. **List specifically what things will happen to the disciples.**

13. **What is the nature of persecution Jesus warned about in Mark 13:9?**

14. **What specific instructions did Jesus give to His disciples as they faced persecution?**

Jesus told His disciples that they would suffer for their association with Him. When people persecute believers in Jesus, it is a demonic, hate driven abhorrence of Truth that drives them forward. It is Jesus they hate – we are merely the visible representation of the One they despise.

15. Mark 13:9-10 is one of the major points to be understood in this section. What did Jesus tell His disciples was one of the purposes of persecution?

16. Why do you think persecution inevitably draws people to Jesus Christ?

17. Does pressure strengthen or weaken you personally?

Desolation, Affliction, Deception (Mark 13:14-23)

Scholars believe this section specifically spoke to the Jewish War (AD 66-70), although there are some who believe this also refers to end times theology.[53] Mark 13:14 is believed to be the oracle Josephus spoke of that later compelled believers to flee Jerusalem to the hills of Pella during the early years before and during the war. Jesus told the people to flee when a sacrilege (entering the Temple) was seen or anticipated. Those who didn't obey the words were helplessly trapped between starvation and violent death.

18. There are six imperatives or commands (Life Alert) given by Jesus in Mark 13:14-23 to those caught in the midst of the war. How many can you find (13:14, 15, 16, 18, 21, 23)?

19. As you read the six commands above, what is the context of each of the commands? (What will happen?)

20. In Mark 13:15-16 Jesus talked about the urgency to flee. How did He describe it?

21. Jesus told about a hindrance to flight in Mark 13:17-18. What was it and what was the remedy for it?

22. In Mark 13:19-20 what reason did Jesus give for flight?

---

[53] Fructenbaum, IBID., 632.

23. **In Mark 13:21-22 what deterrents or things would keep people from fleeing at the right time?**

24. **Summarize what you learned from this lesson in one sentence or thought.**

I have been laboring over this chapter for quite some time and since I do not claim to be a scholar, particularly in the area of prophecy, it has been a challenge to see. I want to be as honest and thorough as my abilities allow as we journey together through this marvelous gospel. And I want to be true to what I believe Jesus is calling us to as His disciples.

I believe Jesus gave these words to His disciples not to scare them or oppress them, but to give them tools to build into their lives *before* things happened so that they could be ready to assist and teach others. Today we are in danger of hoarding the wonderful promises and keeping them from a world that is groaning, oppressed and terrified.

God is looking for people willing to breathe life into others through the hope that lies within. Just as 9/11 was an opportunity for the church to step up to serve and comfort, so these tragically difficult times we live in today are given so that not one would perish. Jeremiah, through the breath of God breathing words into his soul said, "There is hope for your future." (Jeremiah 29:11) This is our opportunity as our faith grows, to deliver to hurting people the power and the presence of God.

Day 2
Life Alert, Part Two (Mark 13:24-37)

Background Information

The section we are studying, also called "the Olivet Discourse" was Jesus' farewell address to His disciples. For almost the last time, He was infusing strength, encouragement, consolation and instruction to the men He would leave behind to become world-changers.

Now we continue on from the previous lesson to seek out the Life Alert keys for the future that Jesus bequeathed to the disciples and to us.

Mark 13:24 seems to begin a new era, one that will happen suddenly with no warning. In earlier verses of chapter 13 Jesus gave clear instructions when to flee and what to expect. Today's lesson is not to "get ready" but to "be ready". Things will happen quickly and the unprepared may lose out. That is why we must be continually growing in our faith and bring others along with us.

We will also see in today's lesson our old friend the fig tree to see how Jesus yet again used it as a teaching tool. Finally, He gave one more parable to sustain the disciples in the arid days and weeks ahead before an infusion of new power would come to propel them into their next step.

Disciples' Perspective

Unbeknownst to them, the disciples were spending their last hours with their Teacher. As He continued to pour into them teachings, commands and instruction, they questioned Jesus, attempting to take in all that He was telling them. Buried within all of the information on what will happen are principles that would help them in their future. As we too continue to seek out those principles or Life Alert keys, they can also help us in our kingdom walk.

Historical Quote

"In every age God has his man (or woman) chosen, predestined and fitted for warfare against the powers of darkness."

- David Otis Fuller

Getting to the Heart of the Matter

Today's Reading: Mark 13:24-37
Parallel Passages: Matt. 24:36-51

The Great Tribulation (Mark 13:24-27)

Some scholars believe this section of Scripture dealing with the end times (which is still to come) encompass the very times you and I may be living in today! Of course, no one knows for sure except the Father, but as we learn to read with the Scriptures in one hand and a newspaper in the other, we too can read the signs of the end times and learn to be ready.

These three verses contain a chilling but exciting picture of some of the occurrences still to come, but with no timeline or indication of when things will take place.

1. **Read the verses and make a list of what Jesus says will happen when He comes again.**

2. End times prophecy is littered throughout the Old and New Testament. Read the following verses and make a note of which verse in the Mark passage is similar: Dan. 7:13-14; 1 Thes. 4:16-18 and 5:1-3; Rev. 1:7-8.

Sign of the Times (Mark 13:28-32)
Read Mark 13:28-32.

3. What two Life Alerts did Jesus give us in these verses?

4. What do the Life Alert Keys tell us about Jesus' second coming?

5. How does Jesus' explanation of the fig tree's growth cycle help us prepare for Jesus' Second Coming?

Therefore, Watch! (Mark 13:33-37)
Read Mark 13:33-37.

6. What are the four final Life Alerts Jesus gave the disciples in these verses?

7. How is being a part of a church like being a servant in charge while the owner is away?

8. What did Jesus tell His disciples about *when* the things He spoke of would occur? What does this communicate to your life?

9. What do you think is the "earthly meaning" in the parable here? (Recall the definition of a parable: A heavenly lesson with an earthly meaning.)

10. Since no one knows the hour, how can you "get ready" for His coming? What steps can you take to prepare?

My husband has been saying for years that we are living in the "age of deceit." It is difficult if not impossible to "see truth" in the news we watch and read, the books we read and the people we count on to tell us the truth. It is perilously difficult to find our way which is why it is so critical to stay involved in studying the Scriptures. I often feel the need to "snuggle up close to the Bible" so I don't get misled. And even then, sometimes I still get off the track and on to a trail leading to nowhere.

In today's lesson, Jesus tells us to be ready – live your life as though He is coming back in the next ten seconds, but dream big, pray big and expect big as though you are invincible until your time here is finished (and you are).

But there is another aspect to the dilemma of "no one knows the hour" of His return. It is part of the "rope of hope." (One word for *hope* in Hebrew is *tiqvah* which means "rope".) J. Sidlow Baxter says it this way: "Again and again, just when the battle seems lost and the situation is as its most hopeless, when the worst has seemed inevitable and God has seemed the least concerned, the Lord has come, the tables have been turned, defeat has given place to victory…"[54] These words comfort me as I push through day after day seeking Him and expecting to hear His Voice. I don't want to miss one second of living in expectation of His coming – whether it is His return as the conquering King or His showing up personally to speak truth into my life.

Day 3
Costly Remembrances (Mark 14:1-11)

Background Information

While the Jewish leaders were plotting and planning Jesus' death, His body was being prepared for burial. Today's story tells about a woman (John 12:3 tells us it is Mary, the sister of Martha and Lazarus from Bethany) who brought a costly vial of perfume to anoint Jesus' head. The vial was thought to have been worth almost a year's wages and some scholars believe it to have been a family heirloom passed down through the generations in her family.

> **When the scribes and Pharisees could not discredit Jesus, they turned to conspiracy, stealth and deceit.**

Jesus indicated that her act of worship would be a memorial, remembered by all future hearers of the Word. Who knew that such a small, seemingly insignificant act which took place in the home of a leper would have such far-reaching impact? And that is the point – we don't know how our words, actions or prayers will impact history or people's lives.

---

[54] Baxter, IBID.

Disciples' Perspective

Three steps forward, two steps back. This described the disciples as they muttered over the *waste* of such a costly gift. (Matt. 26:8) But Jesus and Mary were teaching them something about worship. Just as I shared in an earlier section about my small view of worship and how God was growing it, the disciples were learning too. Worshiping God costs us something. Sometimes it is an attitude within that needs to be spent and changed and sometimes God tugs on us to give financially or offer our time or service for kingdom living. As we see expressed in today's lesson, worship is costly and humbling but it touches God and can affect people for eternity.

Historical Quote

"Keep on because you don't have any idea what fantastic importance your words or your actions or your just being has in the midst of history...Keep on because you have no idea of the enormity of difference your prayers for some one person is going to have in the midst of history."

– Edith Schaeffer, *The Tapestry*

This is one of the most important quotes I have ever read. Early in my Christian walk I came across the quote in an autobiography I was reading. It electrified my thinking and the words went deeply into my soul, impacting me in a way I could never have imagined. It made the subject of prayer come alive to me and others with whom I shared it. Because of this phrase and the belief that somehow prayer makes a difference, over the years, thousands of people have been covered in prayer. And I have been the recipient of countless prayers by others. Our actions, words and prayers spoken or done in obedience can change history, just as the woman's actions in today's story illustrates.

Getting to the Heart of the Matter

Today's Reading: Mark 14:1-11
Parallel Passages: Matt. 26:1-16, Luke 22:1-6, John 12:1-11

Costly Remembrances (Mark 14:1-9)

Read Mark 14:1-9.

1. **In Mark 14:1-2, who was involved in the plot to seize Jesus? What was their plan?**

2. **In Mark 14:3-9, who was present with Jesus at Simon the leper's home?**

> Jesus wants His hearers to do for others exactly what Mary did for Him: to pour out the richness of the gifts that He has given to each of us to anoint, encourage and bless. And surely He wants to pour out the precious perfume on us too. In defining our most abandoned expectation of the future and our own dreams and visions, God wants to bless us, affirm the dream and bestow the gift.

3. We know from other passages that the woman is Mary, Lazarus' sister. What can you learn about her from reading the passage? Write down any observations or facts about her that you see. You might learn more information by reading the parallel passages.

4. How do you define "extravagant worship"? Do you think Mary's actions in Mark 14:3 would be considered worship? Why or why not?

5. What is the most extravagant thing you have done for Jesus? Did you consider it an act of worship?

6. Why were the guests upset with Mary for using such expensive perfume?

In Mark 14:7 Jesus comments about the poor. Isn't it interesting that most of the time people aren't really concerned about the poor or other marginalized groups until they want to criticize someone? It is easy to misread this passage and think that Jesus lacked concern for the poor.

7. From what you have seen of Jesus' life so far, do you agree or disagree with the statement that Jesus was not concerned about the poor?

8. Did Jesus have a message about the poor in Mark 4:7 for His hearers? What was it? (Read Deuteronomy 15:11 for a clue.)

9. It was actually not unusual for Jews to remember the poor with gifts during the Passover. From reading the passage, how was Jesus censuring the disciples?

Judas (Mark 14:10-11)

Read Mark 14:10-11. We haven't learned much about Judas in Mark's gospel though in other gospels we learn that he was the treasurer of the group. (John 13:21-26)

10. **From this passage, what can you learn about Judas' character?**

11. **Do you think Judas' decision in Mark 14:10-11 was impulsive or thought out? Do these verses suggest either theory?**

12. **Jesus was not actually hiding His movements from anyone (except perhaps in the location of the Passover meal). How then could Judas betray Him? What opportunity do you think Judas was looking for? (Clue: What were the religious leaders concerned about in Mark 14:1-2?)**

13. **What differences do you see between Mary and Judas?**

I can't imagine some of the people and disciples griping about wasting a vial of perfume on the Savior can you? And yet, aren't we also guilty of wasting, giving away, selling short what we most value? Do we pour out our gifts to make ourselves wealthy, gain popularity, power or acceptance? Instead of pouring out who we are to serve Him, do we sell ourselves too cheaply to gain something that won't last? A night of pleasure, a white lie to gain something we don't want anyway? A hidden deal that risks exposure and puts our reputation on the line? And for what? Something that won't satisfy in any event!

Kingdom living is about living life in the open and living a life of sacrifice — not always the painful kind of sacrifice that rips people's souls, but the sacrifice of giving our best to the One we love the most. Like the vial, once broken, it filled the room with its fragrance. So is our life a fragrance when poured out for God. Our sacrifices fill the void in someone else's life, and in so doing, may make all the difference to that person.

The woman whose memory lives on because of her sacrificial service is our example. She had no idea of the importance of her gift in preparing Jesus for burial. She didn't understand the importance of what she was doing. She brought what she had and poured it out on Him. And that service impacted eternity. Go and do likewise!

As we finish today's lesson, I want to leave you with two questions to ponder: (1) How can you receive the gift of God's anointing oil in your own life? Just as Mary prepared Jesus for His next step, so God is preparing us for our next step (not necessarily *the same step*). What expectations, hopes and dreams do you have that

God can extravagantly bless in you? (2) How can you be His hands, feet, voice, ear in someone else's life to pour out His oil on others?

Day 4
The Lord's Last Supper (Mark 14:12-31)

Background Information

In today's study there are some poignant lessons as Jesus and His disciples prepare one more time for Passover. This was the yearly festival of national redemption. It signifies God's deliverance of His people from bondage.

Once a year a perfect, spotless male lamb was chosen from the family's flock to live with them for several days before the Passover meal, thus allowing the family time to get to know the lamb. On the afternoon that Passover began (it began at sunset when the meal was to be eaten), the lamb was slain and eaten by the family as a remembrance of God's freeing them from slavery in Egypt.

It was also a reminder that He passed over their first born when He saw the blood of the slain lamb on the doorpost, excluding them from the death that the Egyptian first born sons were subjected to. It is also a picture of how God passes over our own sin when He sees our acceptance of Jesus who represents the blood of the sinless Lamb of God covering our lives.

I wish there were time in this book to give you the background on the beauty of the Passover. The imagery and meaning of every single part of the ceremony is unmistakably all about Him! As He was preparing for the last earthly Passover, I wonder if He was remembering the first Passover. You can read about it in Exodus 12:1-13. How many elements of the ceremony remind you in some way of what you have learned about Jesus thus far?

This was clearly Jesus' last meal. He told His disciples that He would not enjoy food or drink until He experienced it in the kingdom of God. He was anticipating what the next twenty four hours would bring even though the disciples were unaware of it and the impact it would have on their own impending weakness of soul.

Disciples' Perspective

It is quite possible that even during this last meal that Jesus ate with His disciples, they were still unclear about His message to them. In today's passage, we see the disciples getting indignant over the use of a costly perfume to anoint Jesus. Even though Jesus told them again of His upcoming death and burial, there is no indication in the passage that they understood Him. Perhaps it is selective hearing.

I've been known to accuse my own family of such a flaw when I am telling them something I consider important. I've even been known to practice it myself a time or two.

Selective hearing is bad enough when employed with a family member, but another thing entirely to exercise when God is speaking. Growing deeper into the call implies that we are increasingly learning how to listen to Him. Even when we hear things we'd rather not know about, we still need to listen and obey. Perhaps this is why, when Jesus told them at the last meal that one of them would betray Him (Mark 14:18-21) everyone feared he might be the one.

There are times when we all betray Him by failing to listen. If we are honest with ourselves, more often than not, it is because we really don't want to listen!

Historical Quote

"Late have I loved you, O beauty so ancient and so new. Late I have loved you! You were within me while I have gone outside to seek you. Unlovely myself, I rushed towards all those lovely things you had made. And always you were with me and I was not with you. All these beauties kept me far from you – although they would not have existed at all unless they had their being in you. You called, you cried, you shattered my deafness. You sparkled, you blazed, you drove away my blindness. You shed your fragrance and I drew in my breath and I pant for you. I tasted and now I hunger and thirst. You touched me, and now I burn with longing for your peace."

-St. Augustine, *Confessions*

Getting to the Heart of the Matter

Today's Reading: Mark 14:12-31
Parallel Passages: Matt. 26:17-35, Luke 22:7-23, :31-38 John 13:1-30, :36-38

Jesus Arranges the Passover Meal (Mark 14:12-16)

Up to this point, Jesus did not hide His whereabouts from the masses but there is speculation that perhaps He kept the place of the last meal a secret from even the disciples to prevent His last meal with the twelve from being interrupted.

1. **How did Jesus reveal the place where the Passover meal would be taken in Mark 14:13-15?**

Jesus Announces His Betrayer (Mark 14:17-21)

The Passover meal began at 6 p.m. on Thursday (in today's modern calendar). Within 24 hours Jesus would be in the tomb, but not before sharing one more meal with the disciples and exposing one more act of treachery.

2. **Why do you think each disciple was afraid he might be the one who would betray Jesus?**

The First Communion (Mark 14:22-26)
Read Mark 14:22-26.

3. **What is the order of events in Mark 14:22-24?**

4. **What did Jesus mean when He spoke of the cup and the broken bread?**

By reading the parallel passages of the Passover meal (Ex.12:1-13) you will discover that there is much more to the ceremony than Mark describes in his gospel.

5. **Why do you think he gave so little information about the actual Passover meal?**

6. **What do you think Jesus was referring to when He said that He would drink new wine in the kingdom of God?**

7. **Read Mark 14:26. What was the last thing Jesus and the disciples did before leaving to walk to Gethsemane?**

8. **Do you think singing a hymn had any significance for the suffering church Mark was addressing the gospel to?**

Famous Last Words (Mark 14:27-31)
Zech.13:7 is another layered verse that speaks of Israel but is also prophetic of the moment Jesus and His disciples were about to walk into. The verses are a bit confusing, but in the context, God commands that the "Shepherd be struck down that the sheep may be scattered" as an integral part of the refining process which will result in the creation of a new people of God. These verses connect to Zech.

13:1 which describes a "fountain being opened up" to pour out for sin and impurity.[55] The fountain refers to the blood of Christ.

9. **After reading the above paragraph, identify what you see concerning:**

   (a) Jesus

   (b) The disciples

   (c) The future

10. **What was Peter's response in Mark 14:29?**

11. **Look back to Mark 8:32. Compare Peter's response then to now.**

I wish it weren't so but there have been many times in my own life when I have let people down – people who were counting on me or people I tried to stand with and couldn't. It is human nature, isn't it? There are undoubtedly times in your own life when you've experienced the same thing. Also, there are times in each of our lives when we have been betrayed or let down. And we have not only let others down (and they us), but God as well. When that awful feeling comes over me, all I want to do is block it out, forget that it happened, and move on with life.

I can understand Peter's anguish in some ways. The isolation, shame, horror, and the impotent feeling of weakness and frustration with our limitations is all there. It is intricately wrapped up in our humanity. Because we have read the story, we know that Peter will be restored, renewed, strengthened and empowered. But not today! Peter has to walk the lonely, sometimes shameful path to restoration, as we all do.

But God is faithful. Jesus didn't forget Peter. And He doesn't forget you or me. Bring those shameful, painful, jagged pieces and lay them down at the Cross and move on. And as you go, seek to forgive the betrayer in your life. I am not saying it is easy. I carry the baggage of betrayal, abandonment, loss and unmet expectations within my soul too. But we must learn how to allow the ministry of the Pierced Hands to flow over us, through us and out of us so we can find peace and rest for our souls.

---

[55] Lane, IBID., 511.

Day 5
The Garden (Mark 14:32-52)

Personal Illustration

On the day my father died, it began with life as usual. I got a call early in the morning that he had fallen and was being transported to the hospital. I told the nurse I would get there as soon as I could. That day was also the Christmas potluck for 135 women in our Women's Bible Study program meeting in different homes, but leaving their children with us. For me, it was a work day so I went to church to unlock doors, make sure baby-sitters were in place and to direct uninformed women to where their class was meeting.

I was the lone staff person on campus that day as no other staff personnel were available. I remember standing in the parking lot watching the last of the cars depart for their party and I headed off to the hospital not realizing I would never speak to my father again. It was all so normal. Looking back it seems almost horrifying. I had just seen him the day before and he appeared fine. When I got to the hospital (I was alone at the beginning), I was thrust into a confusing world of life-ending decision-making that I was not ready for.

It was the loneliest day of my life. At key moments throughout the day, including when my father actually passed, I was alone. Even though I knew the divine Presence was with me, I still felt a blanket of loneliness covering me so strong, I couldn't sense His Presence. It was a faith step to know He was with me. It was through no fault of anyone. My sister whose husband was out of town had to pick up kids – mine included. No one from church was available. Two of our pastors were in Hawaii, the Administrative Assistant was on vacation, the children's director was out of town, my women leaders were running the Christmas parties and none of my close friends were reachable by phone on that particular day. I felt utterly isolated and alone sitting in the hospital room with nothing but the quiet sounds of the machines surrounding me as my father was slipping into eternity.

I remember being surprised that life went on as usual. People were doing laundry, nurses were hurrying to and fro helping other patients, some people were cleaning their houses, enjoying lunch with a friend, shopping. And my father was dying. How could that be? I am always astonished by the fact that life doesn't stop when someone you love dies. I wonder if any of the disciples or followers of Jesus felt this way?

Background Information

As I have pondered and prayed over these last days of our study of Mark's gospel, I recognize that there are some places you and I just cannot go. I cannot begin to understand the depths of what happened that night in Garden of Gethsemane where Jesus, who from eternity past was in fellowship with the Father and Spirit, was now bereft of all community, all comfort, all help. To not hear His Father's voice as He prayed, or to not experience the moment by moment companionship He was accustomed to was undoubtedly a bewildering experience.

The silence of heaven must have been deafening. Jesus was experiencing total isolation perhaps for the first time in eternity past.

We all have our moments, our "dark nights", our problems but we cannot experience anything near what Jesus faced in the Garden as all of the demons of hell and Satan himself descended on that one, lone location to prevent one isolated, praying Man from choosing that for which He was sent.

We can stand with the disciples bleary-eyed and well-intentioned but we cannot enter in. According to Mark's gospel, the Garden was the place where Jesus prayed three times for the *cup* and the *hour* to pass from Him.

In the Old Testament, the cup is a description of God's poured out wrath and is sometimes titled "the cup of staggering." Jesus knew what the cup signified and in His prayer, He asked to avoid it if at all possible. It was in the Garden where for the first time, Jesus called for Abba (translated, *daddy*) and received silence in return.

It is the turning point of history where Jesus must choose yes to the Father's will or no. The whole outcome of humanity hinged on one word from His lips. History coalesced in the Garden on the night Jesus prayed.

The Garden was also the place where those closest to Him couldn't keep their eyes on Him for one minute. However, even in the midst of His own agonizing pain, Jesus watched over the three who were His most staunch defenders, Peter James and John. His message to them was also a message to us in the midst of mystifying, demonic confusion. Even in the darkest moment in eternity, Jesus is concerned for those He loves.

Once the decision was made, Judas, with a cadre of temple guards descended to arrest Jesus. The Sanhedrin had local authority to arrest Jewish, non-Roman citizens for crimes they believed were committed. Here we see Jesus, who just the day before was preaching in the synagogue, now being apprehended like the most dangerous criminal. Judas performed his last act of betrayal toward the One he had been with for three years. Keep in mind that all of the events of today's study were foreseen and ordained by the Hand of the Father. Even the method of Jesus' arrest was a fulfillment of Scripture.

Disciples' Perspective

Good intentions. We all have them. Sometimes I am amazed at myself for all of the good works I think about doing for people. I am even more amazed at how little I follow through on them. Such was the story of the disciples. In the last study, we found them staunchly defending their intention to stand and fall with Jesus, no matter what! Today we find them napping in the garden while Jesus faced the most daunting challenge of His short life. He asked them to pray[56] and they too had good intentions, but they were overwhelmed with sleep.

In some ways it is understandable. The enemy of our souls did not want them to stay awake and pray for Jesus or themselves. Satan's intention was to isolate them from Jesus and isolate Jesus from every comfort. The enemy intended to focus solely on Jesus to keep Him away from any feeling of relief, security or calm. It was a cosmic showdown and Satan did not want Jesus to fulfill His purpose in coming to earth. The disciples were the unwitting pawns in the celestial drama.

Historical Quote

"What ought one to say then as each hardship comes? I was practicing for this, I was training for this."

- Epicetis (AD 55-135), Greek philosopher living in Rome.

Getting to the Heart of the Matter

Today's Reading: Mark 14:32-52
Parallel Passages: Matt. 26:36-56, Luke 22:39-53, John 18:1-11

Gethsemane (Mark 14:32-42)

Mark recorded that Jesus prayed at least three separate times. At the beginning of His ministry (Mark 1:35), in the middle (Mark 6:46), and in the Garden.

1. **What similarities and differences do you see between the three occasions of Jesus praying?**

    (a) Beginning (Mark 1:35)

    (b) Middle (Mark 6:46)

---

[56] Whether the prayer was to be for themselves or Him is not clear. Scholars are on both sides of the question.

(c) In the Garden (Mark 14:32)

2. **Why do you think Jesus chose Peter, James and John to wait for Him at the entrance of the garden?**

3. **How many times are the words *pray* or *prayer* used in Mark 14:32-42? In each instance, who was praying?**

4. **How did Jesus prepare for His upcoming ordeal?**

5. **How many times did Jesus leave His own meditation to check on His disciples? Why?**

Betrayed, Arrested and Abandoned (Mark 14:43-52)

Read Mark 14:43-52.

6. **In Mark 14:43 who were the members of the arresting party?**

7. **John 18:10 identified the un-named assailant in Mark 14:48-50. What happened to Malthus, the man whose ear was severed as reported in the John passage? (John 18:1-11)**

8. **Read Mark 14:48-50. Jesus said His method of arrest was a fulfillment of Scripture. Read Isa. 53:12. What is Isaiah's prophecy and how is it fulfilled here?**

> The early church fathers believed the naked, fleeing man mentioned in Mark 14:51-52 was actually Mark himself. This story is unique to this gospel.

Overestimating our own spiritual strength is dangerous. From the reading it seems the disciples, at least Peter, James and John, did underestimate their loyalty and ability to stand in the face of Satan's realm.

9. **Review this passage and write down how Jesus warned them against this very thing. How did He model overcoming this area?**

10. **What lessons can you learn about prayer from reading these verses?**

11. **The term used to describe the fleeing man in Mark 14:51-52 indicates a young man of exceptional strength, loyal, faithful, wise and even valiant. Compare this description with Amos 2:16 where the prophet describes the terrible Day of Judgment. What are the similarities in the two passages?**

12. **Review this chapter and jot down one or two principles or concepts to remember.**

We often talk about Jesus' words, "I am the way and the truth and the life. No man comes to the Father except through Me." (John 14:6) However, in a multi-cultural society where people don't want to believe in one way or one truth, those who do are often perceived to be intolerant of others and their beliefs. It is a difficult path to tread. And believers often suffer for their stand on the issue. I wonder if perhaps this isn't a question that Jesus Himself dealt with in the garden. Perhaps He too struggled with the question, "Is there another way? Must I take this cup? Is there another one I can take instead?"

Even in His questioning, He knew it was the only way. He was determined to get to the Cross because He knew that only through that cup of suffering could you and I freely walk away from the curse into new life. The Apostle Paul said it best: "And if Christ has not been raised, your faith is futile; you are dead in your sins."(1 Cor.15:7) Thank God for the Garden; thank God for the Son who voluntarily chose the cup of staggering; thank God for the Cross.

Family Matters

I am recommending two related movies this week:

- *The Passion of the Christ* – a graphic retelling of the crucifixion. Mel Gibson paid a deep, personal price for insisting this movie be made. It has had an incredible impact on the world. I do not recommend this movie for young children. However, as always, it is in your discretion to decide what is best for your family.
- *Changed Lives: Miracles of The Passion* -- an independent film containing true stories of people's lives who were changed by the Mel Gibson film. I found it to be intensely moving.

Chapter 9
The Rope of Hope (Mark 14-16)

Day 1
Accusers and Betrayal (Mark 14:53-72)

Personal Illustration

As an appellate attorney I have seen some pretty crazy trial transcripts. An appellate attorney appeals or challenges what happens at a trial, reviewing both oral testimony and written documents to look for fatal errors in the trial proceedings in order to win a new trial for a client, or to try to uphold what occurred at the trial to preserve the ruling. I have also read some very odd, unsupported rulings by judges. But I will say I have never been exposed to a trial which occurred at night without the presence of critical, legal limitations and restrictions.

Likewise, I have never been called to court on a holiday (or feast day); nor have I read any transcripts where every witness gave conflicting testimony and where every single person including judge, lawyers, jury, witnesses and victims alike knew the testimony was false.

Further, I have never heard of an instance where a person on trial was asked to give self-incriminating testimony as the only credible testimony. And finally, most particularly, I have never read of an arrest or a trial where there were no charges made against a person for a particular crime.

At least up to this point in my career, I have not been exposed to trials where a person was given a death sentence for claiming to *be* somebody rather than being tried for particular crimes allegedly committed. As we explore the last hours of Jesus' life today, we will see the depths of the depravity of the human race.

Background Information

Mark encapsulated the final hours of Jesus' life by recounting seven episodes.[57] I am not a numbers person, but in Biblical parlay, seven is the number of perfection or completion. In Hebrew, seven is *shevah*. It is from the root *savah* which means to be full, satisfied or to have enough.

---

[57] Jesus also uttered seven phrases during His last hours, as described in Matthew 23.

As we join Jesus in His final hours, we are approaching the perfection of His sacrifice on our behalf. Beginning with His arrest and ending with His resurrection, the perfect and complete sacrifice will have been made once for all. The rest is up to us.

Jesus went through two trials in His last hours, though not every detail and every stage of the two trials are recorded in Mark. Jesus faced a religious trial before the Annas, Caiaphas the High Priest and members of the Sanhedrin, and under Roman law, a civil trial before Pontius Pilate and Herod Antipas.

Who were the Judges?

The gospels (not Mark alone) recorded that the four major players in Jesus' trial were men of questionable character. Hendriksen[58] points out, "Greedy serpent-like, vindictive Annas, rude, sly, hypocritical Caiaphas (see John 11:49-50), crafty superstitious, self-seeking Pilate (John 18:29) and immoral, ambitious, superficial Herod Antipas; these were His judges!" Mark mentions only Caiaphas and Pilate.

Caiaphas (identified in Matthew 26:3 as the High Priest) had been in the position for 18 years. (He was the son-in-law of Annas[59] [John 18:13].) He has been characterized as rude, manipulative and opportunistic. He did not understand justice, fairness and insisted on his own way. He craved notice, power and adulation of the people. Jesus had aroused his envy for having garnered all three of those things without trying. (Matthew 27:18)

Pilate was not without his own character flaws having been described as cruel and violent. He was hated by the Jews and he hated them as well. His own violence caused him to be removed from office a few years after sentencing Jesus to death. It is interesting however, that while the Jews found Jesus to be a blasphemer (a capital crime), Pilate found Jesus innocent of any crime.

The Romans

Rome's involvement in Jesus' death came into the picture because the power of the sword was jealously guarded by Rome throughout the entire Roman Empire, but particularly in Judea where rebellion was always brewing. Only Roman officials had the power to determine whether a capital offense resulting in death could be construed against someone.

Rome often refused to get involved in purely religious squabbles such as messianic claims by various contenders. They didn't care about what the myriad of religions were fighting over unless it involved issues of import to Rome. In this instance Pilate suggested to Caiaphas the religious leader, that he give Jesus a trial,

---

[58] Hendriksen, IBID., 607.

[59] Annas was the High Priest from AD 7-14

but Caiaphas declined because the Jews could not condemn Jesus to death without Roman sanction, which was the Sanhedrin's ultimate goal.

The Jewish Leaders

The real reason that Jesus' death was sought was because of His claims to Messiah-ship. The High Priest Caiaphas and the council of the Sanhedrin gnashed their teeth every time they heard a whispered inkling of such a claim. In their thinking, it was for this reason alone that He must die. Such views were truer than they realized because it really was for this reason alone that He had to die.

They did, however, have a problem coming up with a charge against Him, finally settling on the charge of blasphemy which was very loosely defined in those days. Though Jesus didn't say much, what He did say pushed home the truth of His claims giving the religious leaders one claim on which to pursue His death.

The last seven events in Jesus earthly life were:

1. **The arrest (Mark 14:43-52)**
2. **Jesus' arraignment before Jewish authorities (Mark 14:53-65)**
3. **Peter's denial (Mark 14:54, 66-72)**
4. **Jesus before Pilate (Mark 15:1-20)**
5. **Jesus' crucifixion (Mark 15:20-41)**
6. **Jesus' burial (Mark 15:42-47)**
7. **Jesus' Resurrection (Mark 16:1-8)**

The end of yesterday's lesson and today's takes us through the first three of the seven events (noted above). Abandoned by the disciples (except Peter and one other), Jesus stood alone as He was arrested under the cover of darkness, arraigned before Caiaphas and the whole of the Sanhedrin in the middle of the night.

He was spat upon and beaten by them until finally He was brought by the Sanhedrin to Pontius Pilate, the Roman Governor of Jerusalem early Friday morning. Perhaps the most egregious wound however, occurred in the midst of this dreadful night as the daggers of His beloved friend Peter pierced His soul when Peter was heard to curse, swear and deny Jesus' existence. The wounds of a friend indeed prick the soul in a way nothing else can.

Historical Quote

"It's Friday, but Sunday's Comin'." – Dr. Tony Campolo

Getting to the Heart of the Matter

Today's Reading: Mark 14:53-72
Parallel Passages: Matt. 26:57-75, Luke 22:54-71, John 18:12-27

You Be the Judge: What Would Have Been Your Verdict?

As indicated, Jesus actually endured two trials within a few hours of each other. In order to understand the nature of the trials and the evidence presented, let's go through them step by step and evaluate the witnesses, the evidence and the demeanor of the judge and jury.

Jesus' Trial before the Sanhedrin (Mark 14:53-59)

Read Mark 14:53-59.

1. **After Jesus' arrest in the Garden, where was He taken?**

> In court hearings, clever cross examination sometimes buries important questions in a series of minor, seemingly trivial questions in hopes of getting a preferred answer to a critical part in a trial by taking the witness off guard.

2. **Review Mark 14:55-59. As you examine these verses, keep these thoughts in mind: In capital cases (seeking death), condemnation required unanimous, credible evidence of at least two witnesses. If the parties who testified differed from one another even in the most trivial details, they were not considered admissible evidence under Jewish law. Describe the following:**

   (a) **Who was present? (Note that Mark says the whole counsel was present – scholars believe that a quorum of 23 or more were present, but not every member was there.)**

   (b) **What testimony was given against Jesus?**

   (c) **Compare Mark 14:58 with John 2:19-22. What was wrong with the testimony given here?**

   (d) **According to the passage in John 2, what was Jesus really saying?**

   (e) **How do you think it was possible that so many witnesses were available in the middle of the night?**

   (f) **What is your verdict on the testimony of the witnesses?**

Before the High Priest (Mark 14:60-65)

Read Mark 14:60-65.

3. **Why do you think Caiaphas decided to question Jesus himself?**

4. **What answer did Jesus give to Caiaphas' first two questions? Why do you think He remained silent?**

5. **What was the critical question to the whole trial that Caiaphas put before Jesus? How did Jesus answer?**

6. **Read Dan. 1 7:13-14 and Ps. 110:1. What do these verses have to do with Jesus' answer?**

7. **In one sentence, Jesus spoke of His future enthronement and His return as the conquering Messiah. How did the High Priest respond to . Jesus' answer?**

The term "Son of God" was understood by the Jews of Jesus' time to be solely Messianic in nature. Had Jesus refused to answer the question by Caiaphas, they would have had to find another way to bring about His death.

8. **In Mark 14:63-64 the tearing of one's clothes by a High Priest signified he has just heard a blasphemous statement. Do you think his actions here were genuine?**

9. **How would you describe Caiaphas' state of mind during these proceedings?**

10. **Read Lev. 24:16. What does it say about blasphemy? What was Jesus' defense to the claim of blasphemy by the High Priest (Mark 14:64)?**

11. **In Mark 14:64, how did the Council vote? What was the outcome?**

12. **Who is Mark 14:65 referring to and what did they do to Jesus?**

Peter's Denial (Mark 14:54, Mark 14:66-72)

While Jesus was upstairs being beaten and spit upon by religious leaders, one of His own was downstairs waiting for news of the outcome.

13. **What was happening to Peter while Jesus' trial was ongoing?**

14. **How did Peter respond to the questions he was asked?**

15. **The first time the cock crowed, Peter's conscience was not awakened. Read Luke 22:61 for an important fact left out by Mark. What does Luke add?**

16. **How did Peter respond upon hearing the cock's second crow?**

In the midst of this black, dark hour where the forces of hell descended upon Jesus through those who hated Him and sought to destroy Him, it was the wound of a friend that cuts deepest. "Thou art the Christ – I don't even know Him."

We've all been there – moments of great belief when we *know* and moments of deep despair when we deny His very existence. For Peter, it was a moment of exposure. He saw himself as he really was, not as he thought he was – and it broke him. But it also was the beginning of wholeness for him. From Peter we can take heart, for even when we are faithless, Jesus remains faithful.

I don't want you to forget this story, because it is not over yet - there is more. Do you want to know what fuels Peter's future? Stay tuned and in the following sections and you will see. And I pray that you will experience what Peter experienced. Restoration is on the way! Peter was changed by it and he entered a new, deeper realm of kingdom living. It awaits us as well.

Day 2
The Mockery of Heaven (Mark 15:1-20)

Background Information

Jerusalem, especially during feast times was often a cauldron of sedition and plots to overthrow Rome. It was where agitators went to scheme and plan. Always in the minds of Roman leaders was the possibility of a revival of Jewish nationalism, so threats against Rome by her conquered peoples were always taken seriously.

Wherever the governor conducted business was called the Praetorium (Mark 15:16). Here, Pilate (who normally resided in Caesarea) was probably set up at either Herod's Palace, Antonia's Fortress or the Hasmonean Palace while he was in Jerusalem (probably for the Passover).

Because Roman officials began their work at first light, the Sanhedrin was able to take Jesus to Pilate very early in the morning, giving more time for the evil that was afoot to have its day. Today we look at the fourth event in the series of seven we began to look at in the previous day's study.

Keep in mind as you proceed into this section that blasphemy was not a Roman crime, but perhaps because of the agitated climate, Pilate was looking more carefully into charges made. The shallow claim that Jesus was a traitor to Rome was seen as the sham it was by Pilate, but because Jesus was before him, he had to investigate the matter. It is clear from the passage that Pilate wanted to release Jesus, but he got no help from Jesus who refused to speak except when asked about His claim as "King of the Jews."

Pilate was weak and unable to take a stand. Here before him was no man prepared to overthrow Caesar – this bloody, beaten pulp of a man who was meek and silent could not possibly threaten to inaugurate a new regime! So when Pilate was reminded of the custom of releasing a prisoner at Passover, he was certain Jesus would be released. Seeking to shift responsibility, instead he walked into a trap the religious leaders had prepared the crowds for. It was Barabbas the insurrectionist, Barabbas the murderer, Barabbas, whose name means "Son of the father,"[60] the one who deserved to die, who went free. In some ways he is a representative of all of us.

Pilate felt he had no choice. Once condemned, Jesus lost the rights of a man on trial and could then be beaten, ridiculed, mocked and scourged, a fate that was due Barabbas who, because of the choice of the crowd, walked away a free man.

---

[60] Lane, IBID., 554.

Disciples' Perspective

Well, as disciples go, it is you and I on this journey with Jesus. We, along with the four evangelists (Matthew, Mark, Luke and John) are the only ones who can stand on the side lines and see and hear the agony Jesus experienced on this day.

I have experienced tremendous inner resistance to research and write this section. It is not easy to watch someone you love so much die such an egregious and painful death. But so much is at stake here – our eternal destiny depends on Jesus getting to the Cross. Had He died beforehand at the hands of soldiers and others who beat Him mercilessly, it could not have been finished. He willed Himself to live long enough to crawl on to the Cross to finish the job. I find that unbelievable, incredible, incalculable.

Historical Quote

"God is love-hungry for He is constantly pointing me to some dull, dead soul He has never reached and wistfully urges me to help Him reach that stolid, tight, shut mind...all day I see souls dead to God look sadly out of hungry eyes."[61]

-Frank Laubach

Getting to the Heart of the Matter

Today's Reading: Mark 15:1-20
Parallel Passages: Matt. 27:11-32, Luke 23:13-62, John 18:28-39-19:17

Jesus' Trial before Pilot (Mark 15:1-15)

Each evangelist (Matthew, Mark, Luke and John) told his own version of what happened here. Some give more detail than others, though none are in material conflict with the other. Mark gave some detail, but this is a place where you would benefit from reviewing all of the parallel passages to understand the whole story. If you were to do this, you might want to make a chart with categories for (1) Jesus' trial before Pilate; (2) the prisoner exchange; (3) Jesus' treatment by the soldiers up to the crucifixion.

1. **Read Mark 5:1-5. Who was present at Jesus' second trial?**

2. **Read Luke 23:2. What three charges did the religious leaders bring against Jesus?**

---

[61] Frank Laubach, *Letters by a Modern Mystic,* quoted in *Glimpses of God Through the Ages,* Esther Carls Dodgen, Ed. (Peabody: Hendricksen Publishers, 2003), 309

3. Because of the history of insurrection in Jerusalem, Pilate could not ignore the charges made. How did he respond to them?

4. From your reading of Mark 15:1-15, let's do a short biographical study of Pontius Pilate. Make a list of the characteristics of Pilate that you see in this passage. (If you would like to have a more complete character sketch, review the parallel passages for more clues about his character.)

5. From the passage, do you think Pilate wanted to let Jesus go? From what verses or passages do you make the deduction?

6. What did Pilate understand to be the motive of the chief priests in delivering Jesus for crucifixion (Mark 15:11)?

7. How do you describe envy? Based on this verse, what can unbridled envy lead to?

> Consider that Mark's readers might be facing what Jesus faced as He stood before a pagan tribunal to give an account of His *crimes*. It must have given the fledgling church some comfort to know the Lord had gone before them.

8. John's gospel gives us a more detailed report of how Pilate disposed of responsibility for Jesus' life. Review John 19:5-16 and describe how Pilate handled the fate of Jesus.

9. Barabbas means "Son of the father" (Bar-son; Abba-father/daddy). Read Mark 15:7. Describe the man Barabbas. Do you think the meaning of his name is significant in any way? Explain.

10. We don't know what happened to Barabbas, but can you speculate? If it were you and not Barabbas who went free, what do you think you would have experienced, felt or thought about the remarkable twist of affairs that let you go free in place of an innocent man?

Scourging of Jesus (Mark 15:16-20)

11. Who was present at Jesus' scourging?

When Roman soldiers flogged a person, it often led to death. If the person lived, they were crucified after the flogging. It was a horrible punishment. The scourge weapon was a whip made of leather strips embedded with lead or brass and bone chips. Often exposing human flesh as it tore into a person's body, the weapon shredded people's skin leaving them a mass of bruises, welts, and exposed bone. Sometimes veins, arteries and internal organs were exposed as well. It usually took two soldiers to flog a victim, each taking turns from either side of the body. Because of the horrific implication of flogging, Roman citizens were exempt from crucifixion and floggings. See Acts 16:37.

12. As much as we do not want to face it, it is important to understand the depths to which Jesus went to take our place. Describe what the soldiers did to Jesus physically.

13. How was Jesus mocked by the soldiers?

14. Review the following verses and circle the words *led*, *led away*, *brought*, *sent* or derivatives of these words. What do the words say about Jesus (Mark 14:53, 15:1, 15:16, 15:20)?

15. Read Isa. 53:5, 1 Pet. 2:24. What do these verses record about Jesus' experience?

I would much rather tell you that I was on the sidelines throwing palm leaves before the King on Palm Sunday than that I was with the hecklers in the crowd before Pilate calling for Barabbas' release. But unfortunately, like most of us, I have been in both places at times. I can't imagine myself ever knowingly turning my back on Jesus, but then neither did Peter and the other apostles. It seems inconceivable that the crowds in Pilate's day were calling for the release of a known murderer and trouble-maker instead of Jesus Christ.

But then, Barabbas was "son of the father." What a remarkable reminder of why Jesus had to die instead of Barabbas. It was the exact reason He came: To take the place of all of the sons (and daughters) of the Father. Had Jesus been released instead, we would not have the hope that we have today.

I look around at the world today and see the choices we make and I realize that we are still calling for His crucifixion. Every day millions and millions of people crucify Him anew and every day in the lives of hundreds and thousands of people the resurrection comes and people are born anew into His kingdom. I'm convinced He would do it again and again if it would save one more. Our job is to live out His kingdom within so that others will see and reach out for it.

Day 3
The Day God Died (Mark 15:21-47)

Personal Information

Growing up in a western culture has made some of us rather immune to violence in general and Bible stories in particular. For me, even though I did not come to Christ until in my mid-teens, I still had a background of a Christian culture. Things I read in the Scriptures, though foreign to me at first, soon became familiar. I understood the basics about the Cross, redemption, ransom and the ramifications of my choices – either He pays or I pay, as well as many other Biblical concepts.

But for much of the world it is not so. One Christmas I invited a neighbor (from a different culture) over and as she looked around my house, she saw several nativity sets in the room. She asked, "What are these and what do they mean?" Trying not to look shocked, I explained the gospel to her in as simple language as I could. It was my first introduction to the fact that much of the world isn't familiar with Jesus – many consider Christianity a western religion and thus so many people miss out on the life changing relationship that God offers through His Son, Jesus Christ.

Lately I have added to my reading diet more books about missionaries, and other books about people whose lives I admire. While writing this study I came across a book called *In Search of the Source*[62]. The book is about a missionary couple who moved into a tribe in Papua New Guinea to translate the Bible. The group had already heard of Christ through one of their own people in the years preceding. They were told that someone would come to help them understand more. As the

---

[62] Neil Anderson and Hyatt Moore, *In Search of the Source,* (Orlando: Wycliffe Bible Translators, 1999), 151-2.

author described translating the Bible into the Folopa people's native tongue, he talked about difficulties in translation and cultural changes.

It was when they began to discuss Christ's arrest and crucifixion that things became interesting. Throughout the translation process involving many in the village, Jesus was a man the people had come to like and respect. After translating the entire gospel of Luke, the missionary couple showed a film depicting the gospel to the people. The couple were unprepared for the tribe's response to the depiction of the crucifixion. Women began wailing. They didn't understand the concept of acting or that it wasn't actually happening at that moment. They couldn't bear to watch Jesus being nailed to a cross while He was still alive.

The author reports that a silence came over the crowd until they saw the soldiers drive the first nail into Jesus' body. Then the wailing started. "In the end, beneath the clamor, Jesus mouthed the words which we had read at the beginning, 'Father, forgive them, for they do not know what they are doing.' These words, of all, had the most profound effect on those sitting on the floor of the church." Seeing it from these peoples' eyes impacted me too. I had to read this to be reminded anew of what He had done. I had to enter into this most holy moment before being able to write about the "day God died."

Background Information

Bruce Marchiano played the role of Jesus in the movie *Matthew*, a word-for-word depiction of the gospel of Matthew from the New International Version of the Bible. He wrote a book about his experience called *In the Footsteps of Jesus*. I was riveted by his description of the crucifixion, where he realized for the first time what the cost of going to the Cross really involved. He told of the agony, the pain and the horror he felt even in depicting the scene.

But what really spoke to me was his description of Jesus getting to the Cross – that He had to will Himself to live long enough to get there; that if necessary, He would have crawled to the Cross, climbed upon it and submitted to its torture so He could complete His Father's will and purchase our pardon. He knew it was not enough to die *on the way* to the Cross. It had to be *on* the Cross. The terrible Cross – the wonderful Cross.

In this section of our study, Mark gave much detail of the events surrounding the crucifixion. Of the crucifixion itself, all he says is, "And they crucified Him." There is no way that we can even begin to plumb the depths of these short hours in history. Whole books have been written on this topic alone and scholars who have walked with me through this journey have written pages and pages of detailed, substantiated specifics of what occurred. Old Testament Scripture verses were fulfilled in numbers; details concerning the process of crucifixion from ancient writings have been described and witnesses have been discussed in detail. Here, we will just get a taste of what occurred.

In this study we will encounter some of the eye-witnesses of the crucifixion and how it impacted them for the kingdom, for better or worse. We will come face to face with depravity as He was mocked and jeered at, His meager possessions were gambled away at His feet. We will see a Gentile soldier and a Cyrenean Jew whose lives would never be the same. We will review just a few of the myriad of Scripture verses which culminate in this event.

What happened on this day is a like a scene out of some macabre horror movie. It is the day the demons danced. It is the day God died. We must understand that at this very moment, like in the Garden, history coalesces. It is the most important moment in the history of the world. Everyone was present on this day – the demons gleeful, Satan gloating, the angels watching helplessly, His mother, John the disciple, the women and others standing by in mourning. Even nature was on hold during this monumental event.

And the silent Father watched stoically, heart breaking, without intervening or communicating. Good and evil, dark and light. It all came together in these precious moments as Jesus the sinless became Jesus the sin-bearer. Without the Cross, there is no hope of a future for mankind.

Disciples' Perspective

There is just no way to fathom the depths of the Cross – even for those who have followed Him for years. We cannot go that deep or enter in to those moments. Like the women and faithful ones we will meet today, we stand on the sidelines watching, hoping for an eleventh hour save. But in the long run, as disciples, the question we must each individually answer is, "Does it matter?" Does the Cross really matter in your life? Would you live any differently had it not occurred? Frankly, if it doesn't matter, then we have no hope.

Historical Quote

"I simply argue that the Cross be raised again
At the center of the market place
As well as in the steeple of the church
I am recovering the claim that
Jesus was not crucified in a cathedral
Between two candles;
But on a Cross between two thieves;
On a town garbage heap;
At a crossroads of politics so cosmopolitan
That they had to write His title
In Hebrew and in Latin and in Greek…
And at the kind of place where cynics talk smut,
And thieves curse and soldiers gamble.
Because that is where He died,
And that is what He died about.

And that is where Christ's men ought to be,
And what church people ought to be about."
-George MacLeod[63]

"We need to see His passion for us to awaken our passion for Him."
- Jack Hayford

> Ironically, the words thrown at Jesus in Mark 15:31 were true. In order to save others, He could not save Himself.

Getting to the Heart of the Matter

Today's Reading: Mark 15:21-47
Parallel Passages: Matt. 27:33-66, Luke 23:33-56, John 19:17-42

In this lesson we are going to prepare a verse-by-verse review depicting who was present and what was happening in each verse. The panoramic viewpoint will help you understand how important *people* were to Jesus. They were present in droves and all have something to say verbally or non-verbally about Him. The forces of darkness were also present, riding on the backs of their unsuspecting hosts as they jeered and spit and mocked Him. The Father's presence was also expressed in the natural phenomena that occurred during Jesus' last six hours of earthly life.

1. **Read Mark 15:21.**

   (a) Identify the person and his role in the crucifixion

   (b) What must it have been like to look into Jesus' ravaged face and take up His cross for a few short moments?

   (c) How is this act by Simon like our taking up the cross in our own lives?

   (d) What is your cross right now?

Scholars believe that Simon of Cyrene and his sons, Alexander and Rufus were pillars in the early church. The Apostle Paul mentions both sons. The impact of carrying Jesus' cross must have been such an astounding moment that the man and his family were forever changed. Romans 16:13.

2. **Read Mark 15:22. Identify the place mentioned.**

---

[63] Quoted in Chuck Swindoll, Ed. *Tale of the Tardy Oxcart* (Nashville: Word, 1998)

(a) Verse 23: Jewish women, often present at crucifixions, offered a type of narcotic elixir thought to have been mixed with myrrh to deaden pain. How did Jesus respond?

(b) Verse 24: Who is identified here? What did they do? Read Psalm 22:18. How does it correspond to what occurred here?

(c) Verse 25: What time did the crucifixion take place?

(d) Verse 26: The crucified person had to wear a sign designating their crime. What was the crime Jesus allegedly committed?

> In Exodus 10:21-23, darkness symbolizes God's curse upon the people of Egypt. Here it symbolized Jesus becoming the curse for all mankind.

(e) Verses 27-28: Identify the people mentioned in this verse.

(f) Verses 29-30: Record what the bystanders said to Jesus?

(g) Verse 31: Identify the persons present in this verse. What did they say about Jesus?

(h) Verse 32: In addition to the chief priests and scribes, who else was hurling insults at Jesus in this verse? Read Luke 23:42-43. What happened to the two criminals with Him on the Cross?

(i) Verse 33: What time was it and what natural phenomena occurred in this verse? Read Amos 8:9-10. What does it say about *darkness* and *the son*?

Quoting Lane, "The darkening of the sun marks a critical moment in history and emphasizes the eschatological (future end times theology) and cosmic dimensions in Jesus' suffering."[64]

(j) Verse 34: Can you feel the darkness as you read this verse? What time was it? Who was Jesus speaking to? What did He say?

(k) Verses 35-36: Identify who is present here. What did they do?

(l) Verse 37: What happened in this verse? What does Luke 23:46 add?

> The word *excruciating* is a Latin word meaning "out of the cross." *Ex*, "out of" plus *cruciare*, "torment". From *cruciare* comes the word *crux* which means *cross*. In the language of the times, there was no one word that could express the horror of the cross. The word that later came into being to express it was *excruciating*.

(m) Verse 38: The veil being torn in this verse refers to the veil in the Temple between the Holy of Holies and the rest of the Temple. Only the High Priest could enter the Holy of Holies and only one time a year. This event signified a new age – one where Jesus the High Priest had finished the work once and for all and there were now no barriers between Him and us. Read Hebrews 10:19-22. What does your reading of Hebrews add to your understanding of what occurred here?

(n) Verse 39: What happened to the Roman centurion who was undoubtedly present during the actual crucifixion process? What did he say about Jesus in Mark 15:39?

Centurions were non-commissioned officers (like a modern-day Sergeant) who commanded groups of approximately 100 soldiers or more. The gruesome task of

---

[64] Lane, IBID., 571.

The Call to Follow Jesus

crucifixion fell to centurions and their men. Because of the volatility of the region, during feast days Rome moved more troops into Jerusalem.[65]

> (o) Verses 40-41: Identify who was present here. Also, read John 19:25-27. Who else is identified? We will be seeing these women again!

3. **Read Deuteronomy 21:23. What does this add to your understanding of what Jesus was experiencing here?**

4. **What do you think happened to the other disciples?**

5. **Read Psalm 8 and Psalm 22 and make a list of the parallels you see between the passage you studied today and these Psalms.**

Even in His dying, Jesus was all about people. Crucifixions were historically marked by screams of terror and rage, deep shrieks of pain, shouts of despair and writhing, excruciating (see sidebar) agonies by the dying victim. Yet Jesus uttered not a word. No screams, outrage or accusations came from Him. He died as He lived – a suffering servant, dying willingly for those who hated Him. He died exemplifying kingdom living. It certainly convinced one of the thieves on the cross and a lone centurion superintending the crucifixion who had himself perhaps mocked Jesus.

But I am firmly convinced that it was not the Jews or the Romans who crucified Christ, though they were the instruments who brought it about. No, I did. I am the one who pounded in the nails and helped lift up the Cross. The first time this awareness really affected me was when I saw a painting by Ron DiCianni, a favorite artist of mine. The painting shows a picture of a man in a white shirt with tie hanging down. He is leaning at the foot of the Cross, prostrate as if he had just done a monumental, heavy, physical task. In one hand a hammer is at repose, the other hand is thrown over his sweating brow. It was obviously hard work nailing hands and feet to a wooden cross.

The picture clearly expressed the truth that it is you and I who are the ones who nailed Him to the Cross. And it reminds me that the Cross is still with us today. The mental picture stays with me as I make choices in life. Sometimes I am deterred by the thought of hammer in hand; more often than not, I give in to my

---

[65] *Word in Life Study Bible,* IBID., 190.

baser impulses and indulge – and my indulgence costs something in eternity. Not only are there consequences to be borne, but there is the reminder that someone I love so dearly paid with His life for my indulgence.

Just as Bruce Marchiano's estimation of Jesus willing Himself to live, crawling to get to the Cross so He could die for us, so graphically lives on in my mind, so too is the picture of the cost to get there. There is no light-hearted, easy way to trip through this study. Kingdom living demands that we understand what it cost to bring about the kingdom. Blood, sweat, tears and an agonizing, isolated, excruciating death were part of the cost of freedom.

Ask any family member who has given a son, daughter, brother, sister, husband or wife to the cause of freedom. They understand far better than the rest of us what freedom costs. There is no doubt in my mind that though the Father was silent throughout the course of events, there was a tear in heaven as His only Son, out of deep love and grave obedience, went willingly to a once for all, all for one, death. But Tony Campolo's famous sermon title says it all, doesn't it: *It's Friday, but Sunday's Comin'!*

Day 4
A New Day (Mark 15:42-16:20)

Personal Illustration

Hope is one of the most amazing words ever captured in language. But it is a word that was largely unheeded, unused and misunderstood in many ancient cultures. In Greek and Roman times its meaning was shallow. It was generally defined as an expectation or a wish for something with the expectation that it would happen. In many quarters today it is still used that way, but is even more watered down, something like, "a feeling that what is wanted is likely to happen." That's scanty, isn't it?

The resurrection of Jesus Christ rescued the word from obscurity, shallowness and emptiness. Hope to a believer, by contrast is a certainty – not just a wish or an expectation, but a complete and total surety that what is expressed in Scripture will happen. The Bible hums with hope. Old Testament believers had *hope* of a future rescue by Messiah yet to come. We have *hope* of a future because of Jesus the Messiah yet to come *again*. And death holds no terror for those who believe because there is an absolute guarantee based on the character of God who does not lie, that what He says will happen, will happen.

The Hebrew words *miqvah* and *tiqvah* describe hope as a rope or a cord.[66] What an amazing concept when it comes to thinking about the present, the future and life

---

[66] I am indebted to my good friend Karen Soikkeli for her research on these words.

The Call to Follow Jesus

beyond the grave. Grab on to the "rope of hope" which Jesus cast out to us from the empty tomb. He is Risen and because of it you and I have hope for the future. (Jeremiah 29:11)

J. Sidlow Baxter says of hope, "Just as nature, by one of her master-strokes, brings the exquisite butterfly out of the ugly worm, so, by the miracle stroke of His resurrection, our Lord Jesus transfigures that despised word 'hope' into radiance and beauty; for He abolished death, and brought life and immortality to light through the gospel."[67]

Today's background information comes from my research on the Resurrection gathered over a period of several years. I think it is fascinating that people try so hard to disprove the resurrection, though they no doubt instinctively realize that if it is indeed true, a response is required. Otherwise, why bother? Until people are ready to face the consequences of the truth, they will continue to ignore, deny or outright attack those who are committed to the truth of the resurrection.

Background Information

Roman soldiers were very good at killing people. They were world-conquerors and had the best trained soldiers in the world at their disposal. It was their drive, their call. They would be very sure of death before allowing a body to leave their custody because they knew well that their own lives would be forfeited if they failed in their duties.

It was a violent lifestyle, one that had little room for error. After death on a cross the Romans often left the bodies there to rot for days as a sign of disrespect and to deter other criminals. Jews, on the other hand, were required by law to bury dead Jews *before the Sabbath*, which in this case was only three hours away. This may be why Joseph of Arimathea (a member of the Sanhedrin) went immediately to Pilate to request Jesus' body and offered his own tomb as a place for Jesus' burial. Pilate was surprised that Jesus had died so quickly and contacted the centurion (probably the same one mentioned in Mark 15:39) for confirmation. After receiving it, he granted Joseph's request. With help from Nicodemus (also a member of the Sanhedrin), the two quickly prepared Jesus' body for burial and laid Him in Joseph's tomb.

The same women present at the crucifixion planned to come after the Sabbath and prepare the body properly. Joseph was a wealthy, well-known Jewish leader. It is likely that the whereabouts of his tomb was also well known to the people of the day.

Other gospels report the precautions taken by the Roman guards and the Jewish priests alike. The priests at least knew of the prophecy floating around about

---

[67] Baxter, IBID.

Jesus' resurrection and were taking no chances. They requested and were granted additional guard units around the tomb. A guard unit consisted of 14-16 men. Each man was trained to protect six feet of ground in a thirty-five foot radius. Four men were generally placed in front of the area to guard while twelve men slept in a semi circle in front of them with heads pointing inward. They went in four hour shifts. Guards who fell asleep while on duty received the death penalty. Their clothes were set afire with them in it.

According to my research, the stone that was rolled in front of the tomb was made of solid rock weighing approximately 1 ½-2 tons. The entrance to the tomb was four and a half to five feet high. One scholar indicated that, while twenty or fewer men could roll the stone at the entrance down into the groove to close the tomb, it would take more than twenty men to roll it back up to re-open the tomb.

Finally, the stone was covered with a Roman seal. A seal could only be placed on the stone in the presence of the guards left in charge to prevent tampering with the grave's contents. After the guards inspected the tomb and the stone was rolled in place, a cord was stretched across the rock, sealed with clay and stamped with the signet of the Roman government. This was a public testimony that the body was there. There were consequences to breaking the seal which was a fate even worse than crucifixion: upside down crucifixion. Everyone feared breaking the Roman seal. Even the disciples were in hiding during this time.

Early on the morning after the Sabbath the women, however, were more intrepid and arrived to prepare Jesus' body. To their astonishment, they found no soldiers, a broken seal, a rolled away stone and no body! They met a man who told them that "He has risen just as He said." The man then instructed them to tell the disciples *and Peter* what had happened.

You need to understand the role of women in this culture. They had no authority, clout, or credibility. If there was a plot afoot to steal Jesus' body and pretend He had resurrected, the plotters would not have used women as reliable sources in the story. Yet, this is historically the story the church stood by.

As seen in the gospels, Jesus highly valued, respected and loved women. He gave them dignity and empowered them to serve. It is no surprise, then, that it is the women who were charged with the task of spreading the news of the Resurrection. Kingdom living – even from the empty tomb!

Disciples' Perspective

Did you pick up the part of the story where the angel waiting in the tomb charges the women to, "tell the disciples *and Peter*" what had happened? Here is reconciliation, restoration, renewal and amazing love from the other side of the grave.

Most scholars believe that Mark 16 stops at verse 8 and that the additional verses were added later, but what certainly made it into the God-breathed text was to remember Peter! The broken-hearted worm of a man who three times during his Friend's most desperate hour denied His existence, is about to have new life breathed into him. He is about to be given new strength, might and authority through the power of forgiveness.

Historical Quote

"...that God should conquer evil by allowing it to destroy him...the enemy's own power used to defeat him. Satan's craftily orchestrated plot, rolled along according to plan by his agents, Judas, Pilate, Herod and Caiaphas culminated in the death of God...Satan's end was God's means."

- Peter Kreeft, *Making Sense Out of Suffering* (Kreeft 1986)

Getting to the Heart of the Matter

Today's Reading: Mark 16:1-20
Parallel Passages: Matt. 28:1-20 Luke 24:1-53, John 20:1-31, John 21:1-25

Before we begin this section, one thing you will need to know is that some scholars believe that Mark 16 ends with verse 8. Some of your Bibles may not contain verses 9-20 or if they do, there will be a note citing that "some of the oldest manuscripts do not contain verses 9-20." The reasons for the debate are beyond the scope of this book, but for our purposes, I have left all of the verses in the lesson.

He Arose (Mark 16:1-8)

1. **Who went to the tomb? What time did they come?**

2. **Read Luke 24:54-56. What do these verses tell you about what the women brought with them?**

3. **What was the main concern of the women in Mark 16:3?**

4. **On entering the tomb, what did the women see?**

5. **What was the essence of the message given to the women by the man inside the tomb?**

> **Usually about 75 to 80 pounds of spices were used to prepare a body for final burial. The body was covered with myrrh and the spices were glue-like. Then the linen clothes were put on and the body was wrapped like a mummy. The myrrh caused the linen to stick to the body. The spices and grave clothes combined weighed about 92 to 95 pounds.**

6. Who were the women first instructed to go to with the information? Why do you think the phrase *and Peter* was included?

7. What emotions were the women experiencing throughout their trip to the tomb?

8. Read Luke 24:12 and John 21:12-17. Then describe the exchange between Peter and Jesus.

9. How was Peter restored by Jesus (John 12:17)?

Peter was elevated from being a sheep to being a shepherd. His restoration was complete. Jesus exhibited confidence and love in His dealing with Peter and that was all that was needed to secure Peter's own confidence in God's love for him.

10. Perhaps you have had a similar time in life when you were restored to fellowship with God. Describe it here.

He Appeared to Mary Magdalene (Mark 16:9-13)
Read Mark 16:9-13

11. Make a list of all of those to whom Jesus appeared after His resurrection.

12. What was each person or group's response, if Scripture indicates?

The Commission (Mark 16:14-18)
Read Mark 16:14-18.

13. **What did Jesus tell His disciples in Mark 16:14?**

14. **From reading Mark 16:15-18, make a list of each command Jesus gave and note what outcome they would see or experience if they obeyed.**

15. **Do you think these commands are still valid today? Why or why not?**

He Ascended (Mark 16:19-20)
Read Mark 16:19-20.

16. **What does it mean to ascend?**

17. **Once Jesus ascended, what happened to Him?**

18. **What empowered the disciples to go out and preach and perform miracles?**

19. **Is the same power still available today? What does it mean for your life?**

20. **Review this chapter and jot down one or two principles or concepts you would like to remember.**

When Jesus ascended to heaven, He left the keys to the kingdom in the unholy hands of the disciples and the likes of you and me. While we may not do the exact things Jesus expressed to His disciples (it would be unlikely to find me handling serpents, for instance), the words of empowerment are there and we walk not alone. The last verse, Mark 16:20 gave the disciples authority and strength, *when* they went out.

We are not all called to preach, but we are all called to serve using the gifts, talents and abilities He has given to each of us uniquely. The implied promise is that *when* we use our gifts to serve, He will work with us and through us! This has been the message of the entire gospel study, hasn't it? When we implement kingdom living in the world He has placed us in, He will help us, guide us, direct us, lead us, go before us, follow after us, stand beside us and live in us. I find that not only comforting, but life-changing.

Day 5
Putting it All Together

Final Remarks

Well, we've done it! We have gone through the entire gospel of Mark verse by verse. I hope this has been as challenging and life-changing for you as it has been for me. So, now what? We've gotten the entire story from Mark's divinely inspired perspective. We've seen, heard and absorbed Jesus' words as He called the disciples, taught them, prayed over them, led them, rebuked them and loved them. Further:

- We have become familiar with religious people and leaders. We've seen ourselves in the Pharisees, Scribes, Sadducees and other empty souls who could not or would not grasp the kingdom.

- We've become more acquainted with the enemy and the dark side – how he and his minions dogged Jesus' steps, confronted Him at every turn, trying to turn Him away from His call. Through using every tool available, including Jesus' family, outwardly religious but inwardly empty leaders, and even Jesus' own disciples, Satan tried to derail His purpose. And we've seen how he can derail our journey as well if we fail to stay connected to the kingdom and the King.

- We've toiled with the disciples as they have made strides forward only to fall back even further. We've gone with them on their missionary trips, experienced their fears and failures, their joys, their wonder and awe as they came to know and love the One and Only.

- We have considered Jesus. In all of His perfection. And we know that we can never plumb the depths of His character or His love for us. We have observed Him as He prayed, taught, healed, touched and cast out demons.

Now, it's your turn. How have you been affected by Jesus' call on *your* life? For our very last time together in this gospel, let's summarize what it means to be a part of Jesus' kingdom and try to wrap our heads around some principles that will serve us well as we serve Him well in His kingdom.

Historical Quote

"Christianity without the living Christ is inevitably Christianity without discipleship and Christianity without discipleship is always Christianity without Christ. It remains an abstract idea, a myth."

- Dietrich Bonhoeffer

"If I didn't have spiritual faith, I would be a pessimist. But I am an optimist. I've read the last page of the Bible. It's going to turn out all right."

-Thomas Merton

Getting to the Heart of the Matter

1. Review Mark 1:14-15. Rewrite the verses here.

2. What two things are required of a kingdom?

3. Who is your King and who is your ruler?

4. Review Chapter One of this study. Write one thing you want to remember from what you learned in that chapter.

5. Review Chapter Two of this study. Write one thing you want to remember from what you learned in that chapter.

6. Review Chapter Three of this study. Write one thing you want to remember from what you learned in that chapter.

7. Review Chapter Four of this study. Write one thing you want to remember from what you learned in that chapter.

8. Review Chapter Five of this study. Write one thing you want to remember from what you learned in that chapter.

9. **Review Chapter Six of this study. Write one thing you want to remember from what you learned in that chapter.**

10. **Review Chapter Seven of this study. Write one thing you want to remember from what you learned in that chapter.**

11. **Review Chapter Eight of this study. Write one thing you want to remember from what you learned in that chapter.**

12. **Review Chapter Nine of this study. Write one thing you want to remember from what you learned in that chapter.**

In conclusion, how do we sum up kingdom living? To believe in Jesus is to follow Him. To do, in His power, everything He calls us to do – and it won't be the same for all of us. I am a "body-builder". I am passionate about growing believers, helping them to grow in their relationship with Christ and teaching them (as much as I myself know) about kingdom living.   Occasionally I am called to serve in other areas but I know my true call is to teach and empower the body to grow and find their own call.

We are consistently reminded, however, to 'go and tell'. When God brings someone into our lives who is seeking and hungry for truth, we need to answer God's call to speak.

So many people walk away from Christianity today or refuse to consider it because they see a lack of dynamic living in believers. Jesus was the MOST dynamic life changer who has ever walked this planet. *Everyone* whose orbit He entered was changed. Why aren't people changed and challenged when *we* touch their lives? It is a question we should each take to prayer. Perhaps because some of the obstacles we studied in this book dog us: unbelief, un-forgiveness, not trusting Him, to name a few.

I hope, if nothing else, you have learned through this study that believing is not enough. We have to obey Him, live by what He said, learn by how He did it and show our allegiance by serving others as kingdom members.

For some of you, your radical belief in the transforming power of Jesus will be a lightning-rod. Your deepening spirituality may take you to a place never expected. You may:

The Call to Follow Jesus

- Take on wrongs in the culture, move against failing morality, teach abstinence in a climate where it is unpopular.
- Join a political movement, call your senator or congressman to register your dis-satisfaction with the way your state or country is going.
- Be called, as Gladys Aylward or Hyatt Moore were called – to become missionaries in a foreign country.
- To become a fisher of men and evangelize people.
- To be a fish-bowl keeper or a body-builder and serve diligently in your church propping up and praying for others as they move out into their own call.
- Raise your children to carry the banner.
- Care for the helpless, elderly, widows, orphans.
- Help people get and maintain health.

The opportunities are as endless as the infinite God who created us, propels us, loves us and gives us our marching orders. We *can* impact our world for Christ – by not standing down, but by continuing to love and care as we stand. As the world becomes increasingly darker, our little dab of light becomes increasingly more important.

But no matter the call, you must not abandon your own time of entering into Jesus' life and teaching in the Scripture. God calls us, like Jesus, to meditate, pray, learn at His feet. The disciples did not get everything poured into them so they could go – they went, and as they went, life experiences, God's Word and people's prayers and encouragement poured in. Your own time of receiving from God is what will empower you and animate your own outpourings for Him.

Finally brothers and sisters, we must live out our kingdom call in the midst of a broken, twisted world – using whatever tools we have in our tool chest, doing whatever God calls us to do. Most of us won't live radical lives, but some will. Do you pray for those who do? Do you pray for the public figures who are trying to live out their integrated lives in the face of a twisted world? We, the church, must be a healing-center, a safe place for the world's hurting. It is what Jesus did. It is Who He is.

Family Matters

This week I recommend the following:

- Artwork by Ron DiCianni --look up artist Ron DiCianni's artwork and look for the piece described in this chapter's study.
- *To End All Wars* – a movie based on a true story inspired by the life of Captain Ernest Gordon, a prisoner in a Japanese prison camp in Burma.